# Motivation Counts

## Teaching Techniques That Work

**David R. Johnson**

*Dale Seymour Publications*

This book is dedicated to my district administrators in the Nicolet High School District, who recognized, encouraged, and set as a high priority their teachers' active participation in professional organizations and programs. I credit my success in the classroom to these dedicated educational leaders. Thank you, Nicholas P. Cupery and Dr. James O. Reiels.

Project Editor: Beverly Cory
Production Manager: Janet Yearian
Production Coordinator: Leanne Collins
Design Manager: Jeff Kelly
Cover & Cartoon Illustrations: John Johnson

ISBN 0-86651-740-5
Printed in the United States of America
19 20 21 22 23   V036   13 12 11 10 09

Dale Seymour Publications

Pearson Learning Group

**1-800-321-3106**
**www.pearsonlearning.com**

# Contents

*Mathematics education is much more
complicated than you expected,
even though you expected it to be
more complicated than you expected.*

E.G. BEGLE
*Yale University*

# Preface

This is a book about student motivation. One of the greatest challenges faced by the mathematics instructor, whether teaching in an inner-city, suburban, or rural school, is to develop a treasury of teaching methods that will "turn on" students to learning mathematics. This collection of ideas and activities, derived from my 33 years in the classroom, will help you meet this challenge. It includes teaching techniques useful to the beginning and experienced instructor alike—techniques that can help anyone meet the goals established by the National Council of Teachers of Mathematics (NCTM) in their Professional Standards for Teaching Mathematics (1991).

My philosophy of teaching is spelled out in two previous books from Dale Seymour Publications, *Every Minute Counts* (1982) and *Making Minutes Count Even More* (1986). Many of the ideas in those books are extended or enhanced, and occasionally modified, in these pages. Ideally, the reader of *Motivation Counts* will be familiar with my other books, because a background in my general approach to teaching mathematics will make this book more meaningful.

—D.R.J.

# Chapter One

# Motivating through the classroom routine

The traditional class set-up

Understanding how students feel

The new class set-up

Motivation starts at the bell

What friends are for—in math class

End with a bang

Consistency motivates—and so does inconsistency

**What's happening to the rest of the students
while you deal with the four at your desk?**

We probably wouldn't have to work so hard to turn students on to learning if they weren't already turned off. How did it happen? Part of the answer lies in the design of the traditional classroom routine. Watch what happens as we proceed through four days of classes in a routine that is all too familiar to most of us.

## THE FIRST DAY

The bell rings, and I take roll.

Sara is then at my desk, asking for the assignment from yesterday. She was on a field trip—all the art classes went to the Milwaukee Zoo.

Nick is now at the desk asking for help on problem 41.

Katy is behind Nick, requesting the assignment for tomorrow. She will be on a field trip to the Milwaukee Zoo with all the foreign language classes.

I now announce to the students, "Take out your homework." Some days, for variety, I say, "Let's look at the homework."

I discuss the questions asked by students, and look at the clock.

I see that time is running out, so I make a reading assignment, pages 215–218, and tell the students to do exercises 1–15.

The bell rings.

## THE SECOND DAY

The bell rings, and I take roll.

I ask if there are any questions about the reading assignment from yesterday. There are none. (In fact, there hasn't been a question on a reading assignment in the last 33 years.)

I now say, "Let's look at the homework."

Many students shout, "I didn't understand what to do."

I begin to discuss the homework by asking the students what they don't understand.

They don't know.

The bell rings.

## THE THIRD DAY

The bell rings, and I take roll.

Matt is tardy.

I now give my lecture on tardiness. (In fact, I get so involved in tardiness, I forget the day's lesson objective.)

I then try to pick up on the homework discussion from yesterday. However, no student has done anything since yesterday.

At this point I give my lecture on doing homework.

The tardy student now wishes he had been absent for the entire period.

I decide to go back and re-teach the section, but as you probably know by now . . .

The bell rings.

## THE FOURTH DAY

The bell rings, and I take roll.

I begin by reading the homework answers for page 223, 1–21 odd.

I ask for any questions about the homework.

Sara wants to see the solutions to problems 3, 7, 11, 15, 17, 19, and 21.

I provide those solutions at the board.

Nick wants to see problem 16 worked.

I remind Nick that 16 is not an odd-numbered problem. (However, remembering the NCTM standards on connections, I review the definition of odd and even numbers.)

Jim wants to see the solutions to 1, 5, 9, and 13.

I show the solutions to these problems on the board.

Nick wants to know if he would get extra credit for working problem 16.

I now introduce a new topic, and work through three carefully selected examples.

I ask for any questions about the examples. There are none.

Maria asks for the assignment so she can get started right now. (Apparently, she hopes to complete the assignment by the end of the hour, and believes my teaching will have little effect on her understanding of the assignment.)

I now give the students 20 minutes to begin their homework. During this time, 15 students ask individual questions about the assignment.

The bell rings. As the students rush out the door, I announce that if they don't understand the assignment, it will become clearer to them as they work through the exercises.

## *The traditional class set-up*

What sort of preplanning is necessary for classes like the four just described? It really all boils down to a list of tasks, or activities, that I will be doing during class:

1. I will take roll.
2. I will hand back tests, and homework, if any.
3. I will read answers to homework.
4. I will ask for any questions about homework.
5. I will show two or three solutions or exercises for the new lesson.
6. I will give the assignment, being prepared to answer any individual questions.
7. Finally, I will wait for the bell to ring.

Lesson plans for the traditional classroom routine, as you can see from this list, detail *my* activities; they do not include what *the students* should be doing during class. The students? Why, all I expect of them is that they be quiet, be attentive, and do what I tell them to do. After all, I'm the teacher. Right?

Well, there may be a few flaws in this approach. In a recent television interview, a CEO in a major industry cited the main objectives for our schools, as follows:

- Teach problem-solving experiences and skills.
- Teach communication skills.

- Teach students how to learn.
- Teach students how to work effectively as a team member.
- Give students an ability to handle change.

Makes sense; these are all practical skills, applicable to any job. However, it is very obvious that what industry wants, and what the traditional routine offers, are not at all compatible—or even complementary. Industry wants involved, active thinkers who can work together and deal creatively with the unexpected. Yet in the classroom you have just observed, the only time students were somewhat involved was when they worked on their homework—and that involvement may be very questionable.

In my experience, the traditional class period fell into two distinct parts: (1) I would lecture; (2) students would then work on the assignment. It was as if teaching and student involvement could never occur at the same time. I rarely knew if students understood the concept. In fact, I only found that out when I gave a quiz or test. As to *motivating* the students, I thought all I had to say was, "You'd better do your homework, because these topics will be included on the next quiz." If students didn't understand the material I covered, I chided them about the importance of working harder—whatever that meant! I then proceeded to repeat the material through the same lecturing process—getting, of course, the same results. When students were having a lot of trouble, once in a while I would say, "Why don't you come in for some extra help." Yes, there was a time when I really thought this was the appropriate way to teach, and the way to motivate students.

My past experience, and certainly the recent publications by NCTM, attest that the traditional classroom routine is outdated and will not help prepare students in mathematics—or for life in the 21st century. The old teaching techniques produced passive, underachieving students. Making the critical transition from a teacher-centered classroom to a student-centered classroom may seem to be an impossible task. It's easy to talk about, and very difficult to do. After all, the kids aren't interested in learning—they just aren't motivated.

## *Understanding how students feel*

Why aren't our students motivated? And can we actually motivate them just by changing our teaching techniques? If we try to put ourselves in their shoes, and try to understand how they feel, perhaps we will find some clues about how to build motivation into our classroom routines. Here are a few of the reasons students aren't interested in their mathematics classes:

- When they are lectured to, they have no chance to think for themselves or try out their own ideas.
- Sometimes they get so confused, they don't even know what question to ask.
- When they don't understand the material, they believe they *can't* understand it, and give up.
- When we practice "no-pause" questioning, we give them no time to think—so they don't even try.
- Like nearly everyone else on earth, they are scared to be wrong—so they don't feel safe in our classrooms.
- They believe that the teacher doesn't care about individuals within the class.
- When the classroom atmosphere reflects what I term a "low level of concern," nothing seems to matter—work/ don't work, get it/don't get it, try/don't try—it's all the same.
- They see no purpose or value in the material; in particular, they don't see that the concepts are leading to anything useful or purposeful from their point of view.
- They believe mathematics is nothing but the manipulation of meaningless symbols.

Doesn't sound like much fun, does it. Motivating students who feel like this requires more than just telling them to study harder, or to come in for extra help if they need it, or that they'd better learn this material because it will be on the next test. It's a much greater challenge than that.

In a recent book, *Eager to Learn: Helping Children Become Motivated and Love Learning* (San Francisco: Jossey-Bass,

1990), Raymond J. Wlodkowski and Judith H. Jaynes discuss the results of research into finding out what motivates and stimulates students to learn. They point out these hallmarks of a classroom that motivates:

- Students actively participate in learning.
- Students are provided with constant feedback.
- Students have an opportunity to work together.
- Learning is frequently challenging; students are given questions and tasks that make them think.
- The learning relates to student interests, when at all possible.
- Novel and unusual teaching techniques are used in the classroom.
- Rote memory is not the primary route to success in the classroom.

Our challenge: to create a classroom that has every one of these characteristics.

## *The new class set-up*

Pained by the inadequacies of my old class routine, mindful of the needs of industry, and aware of the lack of success many of my students were experiencing, I realized that changes were in order. If my goals were to motivate students to learn mathematics, and to have them achieve success in my class, I needed to make some major changes in both classroom activities and organization. For starters, I made three bottom-line changes in all my classes.

**1. "Teach By Walking Around."** In *Every Minute Counts,* I explain the unparalleled value of a U-shaped seating arrangement for keeping all the students involved in the class. Over the years, I've added one refinement—desks in each arc are grouped by twos (see figure 1). This allows for easy pairing of students during portions of the class period—another change from the standard routine that I discuss later in this chapter.

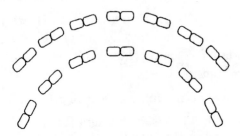

**Figure 1. U-shaped seating with desks in pairs.**

I first tried the U-shaped arrangement because it provided an efficient way to monitor all students' work, by permitting me to walk around the room very quickly, scanning their papers. Eventually, I realized that this seating arrangement was even more powerful than I had given it credit for: It is an arrangement that motivates students. Yes—walking past students frequently during the class period motivates them to participate, motivates them to be involved.

It raises their level of concern. It sends them a strong message: I care about how you are doing during this entire class period. I am checking your understanding frequently while you are in my class. I am checking to see that you are "on task." To paraphrase a bit of popular jargon from the business world, I become a TBWA teacher: I Teach By Walking Around. The U-shaped seating plan is critical to the success of this approach.

**2. A desk-top code, strictly enforced.** The look of students' desk tops as class begins speaks volumes.

Some may be pristine. Where are Tom's math book and notebook? He doesn't know. I asked his parents. They didn't know.

Others show the mark of the dedicated student—of biology, English, world history, French, typing, anything but math. Notice the large area that Colleen has left free for writing.

These examples demonstrate what I dread seeing in my class: students who come to observe, not to participate. Tom has no pencil and paper, no calculator. Colleen is apparently getting ready to pile up all her books so that she can rest her chin on the stack.

Every year, I spell out to students my desk-top rules: They are to have a paper, a pencil, their math notebook, and a calculator on their desk tops at the beginning of the period. Everything else, including gym bag and lunch, should be off the desk. The students get my message: This is going to be a class in which they will be asked to participate frequently, using their notebook, pencils, and calculators.

**Tom's desk—a problem.**

**Colleen's desk—another sort of problem.**

**3. No shouted answers.** It might seem that a classroom sprinkled with eager faces, shouting out answers to my every question, is the perfect model of a motivated class. Not so. The shouters themselves may be motivated, but what about all the rest? So, in the first weeks of every new class, I train the students not to call out answers at any time during the class period. Often this is not an easy task, but the ultimate payoff in total student involvement is worth it.

Instead of calling out, students are told to raise their hands. This way I can give everyone a fair chance—and time to think. I also instruct students to have their paper and pencil ready at all times, and *use* them. That is, many of my questions will call for everyone in the class to write an answer. This way, as I go through my TBWA routine, I can monitor the progress of every student, not just those few who are always first with the answer.

Using paper-and-pencil responses has a number of distinct advantages for me, as teacher:

- It aids in classroom control, because it keeps students involved in a mathematical activity.

- It's a quick way to check how well students understood the homework assignment.

- As I begin to teach a new concept, I can quickly find my students' readiness level.

- It's an efficient way to get feedback on the understanding of a new concept. I receive instant input, and can make instant modification of my teaching techniques.

- As I observe each student's work, I pick up information that helps in planning for the next class period.

- Knowing everyone's level of understanding, I can prevent sending my students home with an inappropriate assignment.

But more important, paper-and-pencil responses are a key motivational tool, keeping all the students engaged in what's going on in my class. With written responses, *every* student participates in *every* question. In particular, nonverbal members of the class have a chance to participate fully. Also, it's safe for my students to be wrong sometimes—nobody is embarrassed by a mistake. In fact, because they are not overcome by the stigma of "being wrong," they often show an increased desire to ask "Why?" when their answer is incorrect.

Those are my three bottom-line classroom techniques: TBWA, the desk-top code, and the emphasis on giving every student a chance to respond to questions. It's not the end and all of motivating the kids in my class, but it's a good start.

## Motivation starts at the bell

Those readers familiar with my other books will recognize another one of my teaching principles, whose power in motivating students is proven: *Start class immediately at the opening bell.* The first few minutes are NOT the time to

- take roll.
- help an individual student on a problem.
- give out an assignment for tomorrow.
- give an assignment to a student who was absent yesterday.
- give an assignment to a student who may be absent tomorrow.
- talk to another staff member.
- hand back homework.
- hand back tests.

These activities are common period-openers in many class-rooms, including—I'm sorry to confess—my own. Even though I know that much important learning could take place in the first part of the class period, this is where I often slot the lowest-level activities.

The first part of the period should be for *all* students. In fact, getting all students involved during the first two minutes of the class period should be my goal. At the beginning of the school year, I inform students that the first part of the period is going to belong to the entire class. In other words, it is NOT a time for individual help, or individual questions. When the bell rings, I will introduce an activity to the entire

—with their desk tops in Ready Mode—they are to
king and working at once. Students on task are
_ivated students!

For each day's class opener, I must plan meaningful
activities that will include everyone. In *Every Minute Counts*
and *Making Minutes Count Even More,* I have detailed a great
number of specific openers and types of activities that get the
ball rolling as soon as the bell rings. Following is just a brief
sample of ideas:

- Review the skills relating to the most-missed question on
  yesterday's test.

- Supply an appropriate SAT or ACT practice question,
  gleaned from sample test booklets.

- Ask students to write the definition of a new word you
  introduced in yesterday's class, including an example or a
  sentence that uses the word properly.

- Ask them to write a brief statement of the purpose of the
  previous night's homework.

- Select a typical homework problem or exercise from
  yesterday's assignment for students to complete.

- Ask a question that reviews material from a previous
  chapter or unit.

- Have several review questions displayed on an overhead
  transparency as students enter the class. This provides an
  instant review for students, and immediate feedback to you.

## *What friends are for—in math class*

The newly popular "cooperative learning" techniques contribute another motivational element to my classroom—one
that you have already seen reflected in the paired desks of
my revised seating arrangement. Working together is a
tremendous confidence booster for most students. For example, when asking a volunteer to place a problem on the
board, I often look for a pair of students, or even a trio.
Reluctant students will be more likely to volunteer if they
don't have to be in front of the class all alone.

Working in pairs is also effective for seat work. Students respond well to the idea that they can help each other learn. My role as the instructor in this situation is to be sure that the task is clear, that each member of the pair knows his or her responsibility, and that both students are participating equally. To help ensure smooth partnerships, I distribute a set of "Student Guidelines for Working in Pairs" and "Student Guidelines for Helping a Friend or Partner," both of which remain in effect throughout the school year. They go like this:

## *Student Guidelines for Working in Pairs*

- At the first pairing, introduce yourselves, learn your partner's name, and find out one interesting bit of information about your partner.

- As you begin, be able to answer, "What are we supposed to find out?" or "What is the question?" or "What is the purpose of our assignment while we are paired?"

- Discuss briefly the question that has been posed, to ensure your understanding and your partner's understanding.

- Share an idea, then ask your partner, "What is your idea?" and "Does my idea seem appropriate?"

- If calculations are involved, work on them separately, then compare answers. If they are different, review the process and find the error.

- Write cooperatively the intermediate steps you used to arrive at the solution. When you have obtained an answer, discuss whether it seems to be appropriate, and if it makes sense.

- You and your partner must be prepared to share with the entire class how you arrived at your solution. Be able to answer the question, "How would you think about that?" Be able, in other words, to verbalize your strategies—that means talking about the strategies in your own words.

## Student Guidelines for Helping
## a Friend or Partner

Suppose a classmate asks you for help with mathematics. That's great! But simply telling someone the answer is rarely helpful. In fact, it shows a lack of concern for your friend or partner, because this approach does not help that person learn techniques to apply to a new situation or problem in the future.

If you really want to help your classmate, you must turn your answer into a mini-teaching experience. Try these responses:

- Ask questions that will lead your partner to the correct solution in a step-by-step approach.

- Give a hint that would help your partner focus on the problem and solution.

- Create a specific example to help illustrate a particular concept.

- Let your partner do most of the writing when you are giving help.

- Ask your partner to verbalize his or her confusion or misunderstanding. In other words, find out exactly where your partner is stuck.

- Once your partner seems to have the answer, ask a follow-up question to check understanding.

- Select an example or non-example to check understanding.

- Whenever appropriate, verbalize your strategies with your partner.

- At the completion of the problem, have your partner summarize the process to check understanding of the question, the process, and the solution.

In other words, be a guide and a leader—not a purveyor of answers and wisdom.

# End with a bang

For keeping students motivated, the last five minutes of class time are just as important as the first five. There are any number of good uses for this time. For example, I can effectively use the closing minutes to check for understanding, to check the effectiveness of my instruction. By monitoring student success with a last-minute exercise, or with a problem similar to the content in the homework, I can prevent students from going home unprepared for the assignment. It's a worthwhile goal to try to send students away from the class having been successful in the final activity of the day. If a student is successful in doing the last exercise or problem in class, that student will be motivated to attempt the homework.

The feedback I obtain during the closing activity will help me plan appropriate teaching strategies for the following day. I can also increase student interest by introducing an intriguing problem, or a problem with a surprising answer. Here's a variety of last-minute challenges to keep students focused on mathematics up to the closing bell:

- List one objective you have learned today.
- List the objectives of today's class.
- List one strategy you have learned that helps with problem solving.
- List one objective about which you believe you need additional clarification or explanation.
- List one possible reason why you learned today's objectives.
- State the major purpose of today's class.
- Write a one- or two-sentence summary of today's class that demonstrates its purpose.
- State one technique you learned today.
- State what you should be able to do as the result of today's class.

## *Consistency motivates—and so does inconsistency*

The new class routine can help keep students motivated, and as I make my daily lesson plans for this routine, I make sure that I am consistent in certain things:

- I will consistently give a daily homework assignment. I will also know who does the daily assignments, and I will know how well each student does them. I will have a consistent penalty for students not attempting the homework. All homework assignments must be completed before I will give a quarter (six-weeks) grade. Failing a homework assignment will not exempt a student from completing the assignment.

- I will consistently determine during each class whether students know or don't know, and will modify the class accordingly—so that I'm neither boring them nor working over their heads.

- I will consistently make it possible for students to ask and respond to questions without fear of failure, or peer embarrassment.

Assuring consistency in these aspects of the class routine will help keep students motivated.

At the same time, inconsistency can be motivating, too. My students should never know *exactly* what to expect when they come to class. Variety in the lessons prevents boredom and inattentiveness. To this end:

- I will vary class openings, class closings, and the order of the activities in between. This includes varying the amount of time spent reviewing the homework.

- I will vary the types of exercises and problem themes. At any time during the period, I may introduce an unusual problem or application to spark their interest. In other words, I don't just save these for when I have a little extra time.

- During any one class period, students can expect to work alone, work in pairs, or work in groups of four. They will sometimes use the computer, sometimes the calculator, sometimes the pencil, and sometimes none of the above. What I ask them to do will vary from day to day, and may include drawing a sketch or building a model.

In these ways, I must be both consistent and inconsistent during each class period. My class must be a place where the unexpected will occur, and the expected will always be present.

The techniques I have shared in this chapter are all part of how I have turned a *teacher-centered* classroom into one that features increased student involvement. Making some critical changes in *my* class period organization and in *my* activities has permitted greater activity on the part of my students— and that alone helps turn them on to what I want them to learn.

*Chapter Two*

# Motivating through good questioning techniques

Artless questions don't count

Being a band director

The pause that motivates

Look, no hands! Now what?

"Are there any questions?"

Smothering students with praise

Mistakes as a route to success

Self-evaluation on questioning

**No questions? It's not always a good sign.**

If we genuinely want to motivate our students, it's time we retired the word "lecture" from our teaching vocabularies. The concepts "lecture" and "student-centered class" are simply incompatible.

How do we teach instead? By asking questions. Whatever my teaching goal for the day, I must never pass up an opportunity to ask a question rather than make a statement. I must try not to tell students anything that they could tell me. This not only keeps up a high level of concern and participation, it prevents me from becoming a lecturer. For example, I might be tempted to say:

"Now, in this equation we add 25 fourths to both sides."

But it would be just as simple and straightforward for me to ask:

"Why do we choose to add 25 fourths to both sides of the equation?"

Or:

"What shall I do next to isolate the $x$ in this equation? Now show me."

After either of these questions, I can walk around the seating ring and look at my students' responses, finding out how much they already know and where my teaching energies should be focused.

If my lessons are to be effective, I need to know at any given time:

1. which students understand.
2. which students do *not* understand.
3. what activities I can best use to find out (1) and (2).
4. what I can do when a student doesn't understand.
5. whether my lesson is appropriate for the level of understanding my students have achieved to date.

Knowing these five things helps me keep my efforts focused during the class period. I also believe that my students are motivated to learn, knowing that I want to know when they do and do not understand a concept. And the best way for me to find out what they do and do not know is through the highly refined art of questioning.

## *Artless questions don't count*

Readers of *Every Minute Counts* will know exactly what I mean about questioning being an art. All questions are not born equal; some questions and styles of questioning simply work better than others. Notice how the following techniques from my less-enlightened past actually promoted nonparticipation and inattentiveness:

- I would ask a question. A student or two would shout out an answer.

- I would direct a question to the entire class. A small group of students would respond.

- I would first call a student's name, and then ask the question.

- I would ask a question, and then immediately call on one student. If the student I called on couldn't answer the question quickly enough, I would immediately turn to another student.

- I would ask a question, and if no one responded, I would give the answer to the question myself.

- After asking a question and receiving a correct answer from a student, I would move on to a new idea—assuming that if one student answered the question, all students could have answered the question.

Do you recognize the drawbacks of these questioning techniques? They allow no time for students to structure a meaningful response. When the question is directed to one student, many other students choose not to even listen to the question. I tend to ask low-level questions more frequently because responses to these come more quickly. Questioning becomes a fearful activity for students—it puts them on the spot. My efforts to check for understanding are inefficient and ineffective, as I get limited feedback about the total class's understanding of the concept.

I also tried another approach in my early years of teaching: I would ask questions from the oral exercises in the textbook, having each student in turn respond to one question.

However, I found that the bulk of the students concentrated only on their particular question, and did not get involved in other students' questions or their answers. As a matter of fact, students were usually relieved when they had completed their response—and closed the book.

## Being a band director

While watching our school band perform in concert, I have always noticed that when the director waves the baton, the entire band responds and participates. The result is a great sound, with 100 percent participation by every band member. Each member has an individual responsibility, and each is actively involved.

Back in my math class, however, I saw that I wasn't working like a band director. Too often, I was directing questions to individual students. As a result, there was little participation and little individual responsibility. I quickly learned I had to be more like a band director, and vowed to treat my questions like the baton: I will always try to direct *all* my questions to *all* my students, and I will train my students to expect this type of questioning. For starters, I made one single little change: I simply stopped using student names with questions. Yes, tough questions and low-level questions alike—all were directed to the entire class.

**Phrases that motivate.** When you're first learning not to call on individual students with each question, it's useful to have a handful of effective ways to start your questions that will encourage all students to participate in the response. Try these:

"Don't raise your hand, just think about a possible answer. I will give you a minute."

"Everyone—picture this figure on your paper. Sketch a possible counterexample to this statement. I will walk around to look at your work, and select three students to share their results with the class."

"Find a counterexample to this statement and
down. In just a minute, I will tell you possibl
check your example, to see if it indeed make
ment false."

"At this time, you and your partner should come up
three conjectures relating to this figure. I want both of you
to be ready to share at least two of your ideas with the
class when I call on your team."

"When you have found an example, raise your hand and I
will come over to look at it."

"Put the next step on your paper, and write a reason to
justify this step. I will be around to check."

"When you have found an example, put your head up."

"When you have drawn the sketch, put your pencil down."

**Phrases that fail to motivate.** I've learned to avoid questions that begin like the following examples. Why? Because I
frequently end up answering my own questions. There are
no responses.

"Does someone know if . . ."

"Can anyone here give me an example of . . ."

"Who knows the difference between . . ."

"Someone tell me the definition of . . ."

"Can someone help me do the next . . ."

"OK, who wants to tell me about . . ."

While these phrases may seem to be opening the question to
the entire class, the big flaw is that they permit most students
NOT to participate. Not one student in the class has to take
the responsibility to develop a response. On occasion, the
top one or two students will respond. More often, no one
responds. So, while waving my baton at the whole class, I
must also take care to construct my questions in a form that
clearly sends the message, "This question is directed to *you*."

An example will clarify. In the implication (A → B), I
might have asked the following question:

"If you know B is false, is (A → B) true or false? Justify your answer."

No response. My next action is as follows:

"Class, on the paper in front of you, write down the implication (A → B). Construct the truth table for this implication."

Then I walk around, giving support to those that need help.

"Now class, compare your table with your partner's. Find the part of the truth table where B is false. With your partner, decide the answer to our question."

At this point—to raise their level of concern even further—I walk around listening to the pairs discussing their results. And I announce:

"I will call on three pairs of students to share their results with the class."

You can see how, one step at a time, I changed a question that was directed at no one in particular into a question that was directed to everyone in the class. Then I guided them to a successful result. In the process, I gained plenty of feedback about how much all the students understood about the implication and its truth table.

**Questions that need enhancing.** These common types of questions need some special care if they are to be useful in math class:

- Yes-no questions.
- True-false questions.
- One-word-answer questions.

These types of questions inhibit the thought process, and answering them is similar to a guessing game. It is impossible for me to check students' reasoning after hearing nothing but the word *true* or the word *no*. When I slip up and ask these types of questions (and I do—we all do), I can enhance them by asking for an explanation. On tests, I will ask students to justify their answers in statement form.

Having students justify their responses, and sharing their thought processes aloud, can be very helpful to other students. Yet, some students are fearful of the little question "why?" They believe it means I want a very formal and organized explanation. Students may even be reluctant to give a short answer, knowing they will be asked to justify it. Replacing the intimidating word "why?" with a more comfortable question or phrase often makes it easier for these students to contribute their conjectures and solutions. Following are some good possible replacements:

Please elaborate.

How did you decide that?

How did you arrive at that?

Elaborate for others in the class, so they can check their thinking.

Can you justify that?

Give us your insights about arriving at the answer.

Tell us how you arrived at that answer.

How did you see that?

How did you reason?

What steps did you take?

Talk to us about it in homespun language.

Tell us more.

Tell us about the process you used.

How did you do that?

What made you think of that?

To a person on the street who doesn't speak "math," tell how you decided that was correct.

## *The pause that motivates*

Possibly the greatest skill within the art of questioning is knowing how to build in a pause at the appropriate time. This means both students and teacher—everyone needs to learn the value of the pause. In a classroom without the pause, only two or three students participate. Low-level questions dominate. The quick thinker is the only active participant. Other students develop a low level of concern. Many even stop listening to the questions altogether, knowing that they won't have time to answer them.

Research such as that done by Mary Budd Rowe, professor of science education at Stanford University, points out some very exciting findings (as mentioned in *Eager to Learn*, cited earlier). In a classroom where both the teacher and the students pause at appropriate times, the length of student responses increases; the number of voluntary and appropriate responses increases; students' confidence increases; weaker students contribute more; there's a greater variety of student responses; discipline problems decrease; and creative responses increase.

The chart in figure 2 has been set up to answer three questions: (1) Who should pause? (2) When? (3) Why? This plan for pausing makes it clear to the class that *all* questions, whether teacher- or student-initiated, are directed to *all* students.

Pausing is not always comfortable. However, I have found that if I never let myself use the name of a student before or after asking a question, my pause is automatic. You might ask, "Well, then, who answers the question?" At this point, I have several options:

1. I could ask that all students write responses on their paper.
2. I could ask student pairs to agree on an answer and write it down, or prepare to give their response orally.
3. I could have each student prepare a response to the question, actually stating, "Take a minute. I will then call on three of you." Or, "Everybody stop and think about this before I call on three of you." Notice that I don't say I will call on just *one* student—the odds of being called on would be too low to keep the level of concern high for all students.
4. Again using student pairs, I could have the student on the left respond orally to the student on the right. I would walk around and listen to these student responses.

| When to pause | Who pauses | Reason for Pausing |
|---|---|---|
| After the teacher asks a question | Teacher | To allow students to hear, comprehend, and formulate a meaningful response |
| After hearing a teacher's question | All students | To have time to comprehend and formulate the answer—preventing a quick, thoughtless response |
| After students have responded to a teacher's question | Teacher | To comprehend the response of students; to allow students to completely finish their response |
| After a student has responded to a teacher's question | All other students | To comprehend the response and to have time to formulate their own response—agreement, disagreement, or enhancement |
| After a student has asked a question | Teacher | To allow other students to comprehend the question; to completely digest the question; and to signal that the student's question is directed to the entire class, as well as the teacher |
| After a student has asked a question | Students | To take time to formulate a response |
| After the teacher *or a student* responds to a student-initiated question | Students and teacher | To allow time for everyone to comprehend the response, and to add enhancements |

**Figure 2. A plan for pausing.**

Any of these approaches, used in conjunction with the pause, will keep students on the ball.

## *Look, no hands! Now what?*

Even though by now I am somewhat proficient in using good questioning techniques, I find there are times when there are no volunteers, no hands—just looks of dismay and confusion. What should I do in this situation? Figure 3 lists some ideas that we've probably all considered at one time or another. Alternatively, I could answer my own questions, and go on. That's certainly efficient. I may be the only one who truly understands the math concept in question, however.

---

### *When Students Don't Understand What I Just Taught, I Might . . .*

Talk louder.

Talk very loudly.

Shout the concept to the students.

Get very excited, talking faster and louder.

Hit the blackboard several times while talking very loud.

Shout the phrase, "Come on, THINK!"

Ask sarcastically, "Who was your math teacher last year?"

Say, "I don't understand you, class. Last year's class got this idea very quickly."

Say, "I think you will get it once you begin your homework."

---

**Figure 3.   Proving that my instincts aren't always right.**

There are several possible reasons why there are no hands:

- No one knows the answer. (A frightening thought!)
- The level of concern is low. (No one cares.)
- The question is not understandable.
- I gave insufficient time for students to formulate an acceptable response.
- The question is too difficult at this stage of the conceptual development.
- No one is confident enough to give a response.
- Students are afraid of being wrong, and of what I might say or do if they give an incorrect response.

When this happens, I immediately switch to working with students in pairs, and include some pencil-and-paper responses. The use of pairs gives all students a safe opportunity to participate. The request for pencil-and-paper responses signals that the question is directed to everyone. As in other situations, my walking around to monitor their written responses definitely raises their level of concern. And the whole process automatically provides time for students to formulate a careful response. In other words, I build in "the pause" for the entire class.

> *Please make it easy and safe*
> *for me to express to you*
> *that I don't understand.*

## "*Are there any questions?*"

It seems obvious—what I need to know in the classroom at all times is this: Do my students understand? And so, after presenting some new material, I ask them: "Are there any questions?" However, it turns out that this is a very ineffective way to find out if the students understand a concept. This type of question, instead of giving me accurate information, actually places the students on the defensive.

I recently observed a teacher who fell into this common trap. After demonstrating a concept or skill at the board, she would turn to the class and say, "Are there any questions?" Frequently, there was no response. She assumed, perhaps conveniently, that all her students did understand, and so proceeded to the next concept or exercise. But that's not what was really taking place. In fact, not all students *did* understand. Some were so confused that they didn't even know what question to ask. They were embarrassed because they didn't understand, and they were unwilling to admit this in front of their peers.

It doesn't matter how we phrase it, it's the same old question:

"How many of you understand that?"

"Who doesn't understand that?"

"Everybody see that?"

"Who wants me to go over that again?"

"Did I go too fast for you?"

Although my goal is to find out if the students understand, asking the question won't get the job done. I need a more effective and reliable manner to check the students' understanding. Once again, using pairs of students and paper-and-pencil responses gives me much more meaningful feedback. Show me! Demonstrate for me! Clarify for me! Discuss for me! Through these activities, I am able to discover how much the students really understand.

Checking for understanding *frequently* during the lesson is also very important. Teaching a large body of material and then checking for understanding may reveal confusion that set in very early in the lesson development—when the difficulty should have been caught and straightened out at once.

I want to emphasize that questioning is a two-way street. If I'm doing all the asking, it's still—to some extent—*my* show. In a truly student-centered class, students are asking questions all the time. Therefore, I want to make it easy for

students in my class to ask questions. In fa‹
convey that I truly desire that they ask que
ask for questions this way:

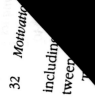

"Are there any questions?"

"Do you have any questions?"

"You don't have any questions, do yoυ

Instead, I ask for questions this way:

"What questions do you have?"

"Now, ask me some questions."

"Now, what questions may I answer?"

"Give me your questions."

Notice the subtle difference. The first set sounds as if I *don't* want questions; the second set clearly implies that I both *want* and *expect* questions.

And then, when students do ask, I must resist the temptation to show how smart I am with a quick answer. To keep the class student-centered:

- Students should practice directing questions to other students—not only to the teacher.

- The teacher should pause to permit other students to develop an answer to the question—not immediately jump in and answer the question.

- The teacher should remind students that the question is for all members of the class.

- To ensure that they focus on it, students might write down the question in their notes. They could then write a possible solution or response to the question.

All of these techniques will help turn students into active communicators, active learners, active problem solvers—the sort of people industry is looking for.

**Asking for help one-on-one.** No matter how well I monitor my students during class and encourage questions while they develop an understanding of the lesson, I also need to provide time when they can ask for individual assistance. I try to make this time available several times during the day—

before and after school. Even the brief time be-
periods can be useful for short questions.

elling a student, "I don't have time now, see me later,"
nay be a turn-off. Chances are, that student won't make the
effort to come back "later." Frequently, I've found, a student's
question can be answered in 10 or 15 seconds. Sometimes
they need only minor clarification of one concept. There is
no reason to make a great big deal out of receiving extra
help. Being available outside of class to answer questions
also shows the students that I really want every one of them
to succeed, and that I am interested in their ideas and con-
cerns. In fact, taking questions outside of class may well give
me direction as to what I need to reemphasize during the
next class period.

## Smothering students with praise

Certain teacher comments, following a student's response to
a question, at first appear to be very positive:

"That's good!"

"Fine."

"OK!"

"Nice response."

However, praise can be inappropriate and detrimental to the
art of questioning and to the development of student involvement. In fact, praise is frequently overdone to the point that
the routine complimentary statement means nothing to the
students. Some don't want to receive undeserved praise.
Other students feel uneasy in front of their peers when praised.

Inappropriate or overdone praise during the class period
can result in several problems: It can put a damper on
student interaction. It can discourage students from listening
to other students' responses. And, it promotes teacher-to-
student communication at the expense of the development of
student-to-student discourse.

Let's examine a classroom incident to see what I'm talking
about. I ask a question; a student responds. At the instant
that the student completes the response, I comment, "Good!"

That "good" just closed the conversation that the question started. That "good" just placed the official blessing on the response. All students have received the signal that the given answer is the one I was looking for, and there is no further need to question, analyze, or enhance the response. In fact, the praise often comes so quickly that students don't have time to even process the original student's response. I have just promoted nonparticipation. Students soon learn that there's no need to listen to other student's ideas, since the teacher will do the immediate evaluation of any response.

What have I been doing to correct this unhappy situation? This is what I try: I rarely make any judgment immediately following a student's response. I rarely react to a student's response with a complimentary phrase. I remind myself after any student's response to *stop*, to *pause*. This implies to everyone in the class that the student's response is for them as well as for me. Frequently, a student's response can stand on its own merit. That is, the other students will recognize the answer as appropriate without confirmation from me.

**Excessive praise has certain drawbacks.**

I also try using the following statements, which I believe are good replacements for my past "goods" and "greats":

"Tell us how you arrived at that."

"Can you enhance your answer with more detail?"

"Why do you believe this is correct?"

"Does this work with negative integers?"

"Is this like anything that you solved earlier in this class?"

"How did you ever think of that?"

"Is there another way you could have arrived at the same answer?"

"What do you believe we must add to Justin's answer to cover all cases?"

"Could you tell me what would happen if we made $x$ larger than 6?"

"I want everyone to think about Karen's response, and be ready to repeat, in your own words, her answer."

"Now that you have heard Matt's response, I want you to develop your own response to this question."

"How was your solution similar to the one Jenny just shared with us?"

"We have just heard Maya's answer. I would like you now, in your own words, to write her conclusion in your notes."

Research like that of Dr. Mary Budd Rowe and others on the subject of praise has found that when it is used too often, students may get an unrealistic and distorted impression of their ability. They move their eyes more—checking to see if they are right. In fact, students frequently check for teacher approval, and fear receiving negative or even just "less-positive" reinforcement. They offer few alternative explanations—happy to rest with the answer that earned the praise. And, because the teacher-student interaction is where the rewards lie, their reaction to other students' responses is minimal.

By reducing the use of verbal rewards, students engage in more self-directive behavior; they participate in speculation and reasoning; they learn that thinking takes time; and they begin to listen to other students.

Of course, there are times when it is perfectly appropriate to compliment a student on a response. However, we must be very careful that in smothering students with praise, we do not smother student participation.

## *Mistakes as a route to success*

The flip side of the praise coin is how to respond to students' mistakes. My actions, reactions, and attitude in class must convey a consistent message:

MAKING MISTAKES IS A NATURAL PART
OF LEARNING MATHEMATICS.

Mistakes will be made. They will be made on the homework, on tests, in class discussions, and during group projects. Students must be trained to recognize and accept errors—both their own and other students'. Making fun of or laughing at other students' answers will not be a part of the class. I must always try my best not to fault students in front of their peers in a way that humiliates, hurts, or embarrasses. It must be safe for students to make an error at any time during the class period.

Over time, I teach students that when they make an error, they must "shake it off"—but only after turning it into a learning experience. Mistakes are one route to achieving success. Here's how:

- The mistake in the solution or activity must be clearly identified and recognized by both the erring student and fellow students.

- The erring student must be encouraged to recall and analyze the thought process that led to the incorrect response. While this is happening, I must be sure that I fully understand the thought process that led to the incorrect results. That is the only way I can help.

- Finally, the student should be helped to rethink, reconceptualize, or reconstruct a new approach.

Both students and the teacher can and should be a part of this process, a process that turns any error into a learning experience.

*Encourage,*
*but not by stating to me*
*that it's easy.*

## *Self-evaluation on questioning*

Following is a self-evaluation checklist on questioning techniques. Try it weekly. If your answers to every question aren't YES, there's room for improvement.

### During the class period:

☐ 1. Do I call on females as well as males for the tough questions?

☐ 2. Do I pause before calling on a specific student?

☐ 3. Do I ask questions without including a specific student's name?

☐ 4. Do I pause before responding to a student's question?

☐ 5. Do I pause after a student gives a response to my question?

☐ 6. Do I call on a large number of students during the class period?

☐ 7. Do I allow all the students to consider the answers to high-level questions before I call on one student?

☐ 8. Do I use student pairs to arrive at solutions or discuss a student's response?

☐ 9. Do I direct all my questions to ALL students?

☐ 10. Do I field appropriate student questions back to the class?

☐ 11. Do I ask students to justify their answers so that their fellow students can learn from the response?

☐ 12. Do I allow students to complete their answer before jumping in?

☐ 13. Do I ask students to enhance their answer when it is not complete, or if I can't tell if they understood the concept?

☐ 14. Do I allow students to respond to another student's responses before I make a comment myself?

☐ 15. Do I avoid yes-and-no questions?

☐ 16. Do I avoid true-false questions?

☐ 17. Do I avoid one-word-answer questions?

☐ 18. Do I avoid asking questions similar to "Do you have any questions?"

☐ 19. Do I avoid using questions as a disciplinary tool, or to capture attention?

☐ 20. Do I avoid group responses to questions?

☐ 21. Do I avoid asking and then immediately answering questions myself?

☐ 22. Do I help a student to enhance his or her answer?

☐ 23. Does my questioning give me meaningful input about the students' understanding of the concepts being taught?

☐ 24. Do I allow students to think and organize their ideas before asking them to respond in front of the entire class?

☐ 25. Do I create a classroom atmosphere that makes it safe for students to be wrong?

☐ 26. Are my students properly trained to act maturely when a student gives a wrong response?

☐ 27. Do I avoid asking only top students high-level questions?

☐ 28. Do my questions promote total student involvement, or do they inhibit student involvement?

☐ 29. Do my questioning techniques raise the level of concern (but not fear) in my class?

☐ 30. When there are only a few hands raised to respond to a question, do I provide alternative ways to respond in order to get more students to participate?

☐ 31. When only one student can answer a question, do I use this input and help others to understand and become involved in the question?

☐ 32. Do I allow students to discuss ideas with their partners before asking a particular student to share ideas with the entire class?

☐ 33.  Do I avoid calling out a name of a student before I ask a question?

☐ 34.  Do I avoid asking questions and then immediately calling on a student?

☐ 35.  Do I frequently walk around and monitor students' pencil-and-paper responses?

☐ 36.  Do my questions help me significantly in my goal *to know who knows and who doesn't know?*

☐ 37.  Do my questions help me learn the source of misunderstanding, or clarify any lack of understanding?

The pursuit of excellence is never-ending, and I remind myself at regular intervals:

I can't be satisfied with one or two students answering all my questions.

I can't be satisfied with one-third of the class answering all my questions.

I can't be satisfied with a quick-thinker shouting out all the answers, and be led to believe that all students could do the same.

I can't be satisfied if I don't know who knows and who doesn't know.

I can't be satisfied until I can help my students themselves recognize when they know, and when they don't know.

"I thought I understood the unit, until I got my test back," Matt says.

I reply, "I thought you understood, too, Matt. You didn't ask any questions. I was so surprised when you did poorly on the test."

This is a sad conversation. It reflects a real lack of meeting my goals as a teacher. Neither Matt nor I knew until the test was corrected that he did not understand the objectives from the past four days. Conversations like this will be a thing of the past if I build on my goals and design a classroom period that is student-centered.

### Reader Exercise

Here's a little activity you can use to see how well you understand the art of questioning. Briefly explain why each of the following questions is of questionable value.

1. Chris, what is the name of this triangle?

2. This is a right triangle, isn't it?

3. Which one is greater, Kim?

4. Who will describe this trapezoid?

5. Is this true or false?

6. Is this a right angle?

7. How does a triangle differ from a parallelogram?

8. $\overline{AB}$ is perpendicular to $\overline{CB}$ because of what theorem?

9. Class, what is the opposite of $-5^2$?

10. What is $(-8^2)$, everybody?

11. What is my next step in solving this equation?

12. Who can help me finish this equation?

13. Can anybody give me directions as to what to do next?

14. Who knows what this is?

15. What is $\sqrt{144}$, class?

16. Does everybody understand the quadratic formula?

17. Is $\dfrac{22}{7} = \pi$?

18. Is Richard right or wrong?

19. $x(2x) = 2x^2$, isn't it?

20. Who sees this?

**How do my questions rate?** Another sort of self-evaluation that I need to do regularly is a check on the quality of my questions. That is, am I asking *good* questions, or am I just asking questions because I think I should? Just asking questions is not enough to ensure that this activity is worth-while—to me *or* my students. If the questions don't lead students to learn a concept, or help me check student understanding of the concept, they probably shouldn't be asked. I must not waste my students' time by asking questions that would be better made in statement form. For example, in a calculus class where the students are simplifying a complex expression, asking "What's $3x + 2x$?" doesn't tell me *anything* about my student's understanding of calculus. Certainly, anyone in that class could answer "$5x$" with little thought.

Each time I ask a question, I should silently ask myself the following:

- Did I learn something about my students by asking this question?

- Did my question test students' understanding of the concept?

- Did my question help students solidify the concept?

- Was my question diagnostic in nature?

- Did my question lead me to follow up with a higher-level question?

- Did my question arouse curiosity?

- Did my question promote interest?

- Did my question tell me something about my students' level of comprehension that I didn't know before I asked it?

- Was my question *really* a question to be answered rather than a rhetorical question, a lecture masquerading as a question?

- Was my question really a check of the students' understanding rather than a technique for discipline or to gain attentiveness?

- Was the question high-level enough to check for understanding rather than just the students' memory?

Questions are effective and worth including in my lessons only if they meet one or more of these criteria. If they don't, why would I want to ask them?

*Chapter Three*

# Motivating through homework and tests

**Tests and homework—not intrinsically motivational.**

If I polled any of my math classes in any given year, asking students to name their favorite aspect of the class, it is highly unlikely that either "homework" or "the tests" would receive mention. In fact, it is a long-standing tradition among the student population to groan and complain when homework assignments or tests are announced. Nonetheless, a few simple guidelines can turn both homework and testing into positive experiences for both students and teachers.

## *Guidelines for making homework assignments*

As mentioned in the first chapter, the key to homework assignments is *consistency*. From Day One of class, inform students that homework is to be part of each lesson. Then make a point of giving homework assignments daily when appropriate, including Friday.

Avoid making homework assignments a penalty. Don't be tempted to make statements such as: "No homework for tomorrow, you've been such a well-behaved class." Or, "I am going to ask that you do all the exercises for tomorrow, rather than just the odd-numbered problems, because we didn't have a very good week." This sort of approach places homework assignments in a very negative light. Students begin to think that homework is unrelated to learning, and that it is only given when things aren't going well in class. Instead, homework must be neutral. Homework has nothing to do with behavior, or the time of the week, or success or failure. Homework is a part of learning in the course.

> *There is an added challenge for you when you insist that homework be done every day by all students: Students must be capable of doing the homework before they leave class.*

Provide practice with in-class exercises before giving the assignment. This creates the opportunity to check students' understanding and ensure that the assignment is appropriate. During in-class exercises, be sure to provide models or samples of the format you expect students to use in their homework. Inform your students that credit for homework is given *only when they show their work.*

Look through the exercises ahead of time. If you plan to assign only odd-numbered problems, make sure that distributive practice is given on all concepts. Also try to anticipate difficulties, and give appropriate instruction so that students can be successful in mastering these difficulties.

Allow enough time in class to give the assignment; don't wait until the last minute. Also be sure to give clear directions. For example: "You must justify your solutions to all exercises and problems in an organized format." At the same time, make the purpose of the homework obvious. You can even have students write the objective of the homework assignment at the top of their paper before beginning the work. It will help them bring focus and purpose to their assignment. If reading is part of the assignment, provide a reading guide. Take the time in class to discuss and clarify new vocabulary needed to understand the reading.

One key to a good homework assignment is that it always be *clearly defined.* I must avoid these tempting traps:

- Optional assignments.

- Vague assignments.

- "Please-look-over" assignments.

- Reading assignments without specific directions or a reading guide.

- "Try-a-couple-of-each" assignments.

- "Until-you-understand" assignments.

- "Work-a-couple-from-each-section" assignments.

Assignments of this sort lack specificity, and very few students can handle them. A few *very good* students will work all of the problems; most others will assume that it really wasn't an assignment that you expected them to write out. Making very specific, concise, purposeful assignments will produce more effective results and will make it more likely that students will complete the homework happily and confidently.

## *Homework: The morning after*

"Are there any questions on the homework?"

Sara's hand goes up instantly! She wants to see the solutions to problems 2, 3, 6, 9, and 13.

The issue of how to go over homework without losing half the students in the bargain has long been troublesome for me. Early in my career, I would have diligently worked out problems 2, 3, 6, 9 and 13 for the entire class, failing to observe that I was the only person actively involved. Some students may have watched my performance. Others would become very inattentive. Even Sara would no longer be paying attention by the time I reached the solution for number 13!

Then I had an idea—a way to get more student involvement in the process. I'd ask for volunteers to place the solutions on the board and explain their steps.

"Who will do number 2? Thanks, Rich. Number 3? Katie, you got it. Number 6? Lynnelle, it's yours. Number 9— Scott, you take that one. Number 13? Anyone? OK! I'll do it myself."

So Rich, Katie, Lynnelle, and Scott go to the board and write their solutions. The rest of the students watch or fidget. Rich begins to read his steps and sits down. Kate, Lynnelle, and Scott then read their solutions.

Did I increase student involvement? Hardly! Only one student was involved at a time. All other students just listened—or did they? I found that having students present their solutions to homework exercises was no more effective than having me present the solutions. TALKING IS TALKING, NO MATTER WHO IS DOING IT! In fact, students frequently gave their solutions so fast that most of the others gained very little from the experience. My goal to involve more students in homework review was not reached. As evidence of what a bad idea it was, there were times I would follow up the above activity by asking students to do a similar exercise, and no one could do it. Going over homework in this manner not only fails to increase participation and motivation, it doesn't help a soul.

---

*Watching and listening to fellow students explain homework solutions does not enhance my understanding of the skill or concept.*

---

Is there any way at all to promote total student involvement during the "going-over-the-homework" portion of the class period? Yes! Here's my new plan of action: I can *ask questions* and *give directions* rather than *telling* the steps to take.

To keep myself on track, I limit the number of statements I allow myself to make while going over the homework. Replacing my statements with questions and directions turns homework review into a student-centered activity. At the same time, I encourage my students to ask questions and give directions when *they* explain a homework solution, too.

"What theorem justifies my next step?"

"What is the measure of this angle?"

"What error have I made in this step?"

"How did I know that this expression is undefined?"

"At what values of $x$ is the expression undefined?"

"What step do I do next?"

"Locate angle $A$ on your diagram."

"Mark the corresponding sides on your papers."

"Think of a counterexample and write it on your paper."

"Do the next step on your paper."

"Complete the problem with your partner."

When we're going over a particular problem, I ask students to turn over their homework and rework the problem on the back as the questions and directions are given. As during other class activities, I direct all questions to all students. And when a student is explaining a problem, that student must also direct all questions to all students.

I ask student volunteers not to write the entire solution on the board when they begin, but to complete the solution step by step as they give directions and questions. This procedure builds in an automatic pause for all students, while the student at the board is writing. This gives them time to comprehend the method of solution, or even more important, time to complete the solution on their own.

The same process can be extended to having several students working at the board at the same time, each with different exercises. Other students can select the exercise explanations in which they wish to participate. During any of these procedures, students are not permitted to copy another student's work from the board. Instead, they are directed to attempt their own solutions at their seats. I try to discuss only a couple of requested exercises in this manner before I have a follow-up activity for all students. This immediate feedback gives me an indication of the effectiveness of discussing the two homework exercises.

> *Copying down the homework*
> *solutions from the board*
> *is a totally ineffective way*
> *for me to learn the*
> *related concepts and skills.*

Here are some other thoughts on dealing with homework the morning after. Sometimes I collect only one or two of the problems from an assignment. This gives me enough feedback to determine whether students understand the concepts. It also saves time, time that I can use more productively in preparing for the next class period.

Sometimes I pair up students to check their homework. I ask them to compare solutions and approaches. I walk around monitoring the work and helping out as needed.

When certain problems gave everyone trouble, I make a point to provide additional practice and instruction. Then I reassign those same problems that everyone missed as part of the next day's homework. This allows students more time, and sends the message that they are responsible for working out all problems.

> *There is no guarantee that, after watching the solution of ten homework problems or excersises, I will be able to solve the eleventh problem.*

## A testing plan for long-term learning

Like homework, tests are a fact of life in my math classes. I'm always going to give them—that will not change. (I do, however, try not to say "end-of-chapter" or "end-of-unit" when referring to tests—this only reinforces the belief of many students that mathematics is organized by chapters.) What *can* change is the attitude students have about tests. They need to understand that I am not "out to get them" with my tests. I want my students to be successful on a test, and I do everything in my power to assure that they will be.

For one thing, I announce the test date well in advance of the actual test day. Surprise tests and quizzes are negative experiences. In fact, some students actually interpret surprise tests as a way for the teacher to catch them off guard and unprepared. It's naive for me to think that all students will be prepared in all subjects, every day, to the degree that they could do well on a test or quiz. I have found very few students who could ever be that disciplined, or had the time each day for such preparation.

As a matter of routine, I give a test every Friday, usually not for the full period. Each Friday test has items pertinent to what we studied the first four days of the week. Each test also has items that relate to material from past weeks. I always try to include a question similar to one most missed on the previous Friday's test. This is no secret; I inform my students that I will do this on all tests. This technique motivates students to review concepts they had trouble with on past tests. It also gives them the advantage of knowing the content of at least one question on the next test.

Besides being clear about when the tests will be and what they will cover, I take responsibility for teaching my students *how to prepare* for tests. This actually starts long before the word "test" ever comes up—when I teach them how to take good class notes.

**There's no need for tests to be threatening.**

**Note taking is a learned skill.** For my students to develop the skill of note taking, I need to teach note-taking techniques during each period throughout the year. I explain my preferred notebook system and the periodic evaluation of the students' notebooks in *Every Minute Counts*. Briefly:

- At the beginning of every period, I insist that notebooks be on the students' desks, open.

- I demonstrate how to take notes by showing models and samples of daily notes taken by students in previous classes.

- I have students write the daily objective at the top of their notes.

- During class, I help students know when to take notes by giving a signal when to write, and when not to write. I also give students a signal that lets them know *what* to write.

- I always have students include tricky or difficult parts of a concept ("critical attributes") in their notes.

- I monitor the note-taking process by walking around during the class period.

- I ask students to highlight key ideas at the end of the class period, and to write a summary of the day's lesson at the end of their notes.

- I have students develop a master vocabulary list from their notes, including definitions and examples, and counterexamples to support and to clarify definitions.

## *My role in student test preparation*

Having good notes from class is a great foundation for studying for tests, but even with good notes, students don't automatically know how to go about the task. For this reason, I always hand out a study guide ("How to Study for a Test," *Every Minute Counts,* p. 56). However, my responsibility goes beyond providing a list of procedures for self-study. I must model test preparation—as should you. Who else! After all, you and I were successful in learning mathematics.

We need to share with our students how we gained our understanding.

Through trial and error, I found a number of classroom activities that were NOT sufficient to help students prepare for tests. For example, at the beginning of the period, I would have students complete the chapter review in the textbook while I would remain at my desk waiting for questions. Or, I might assign students to work in groups for the entire period, doing only test review. Sometimes, I would simply announce that there would be a test tomorrow, and let the students study independently for the remainder of the period—if they were so motivated! However well-meant, these activities lacked the direction that the students needed. I was assuming, of course, that most students knew how to study for a math test; in a sense, I was also telling students that it was up to them to figure out what I might hold them accountable for.

Because I want my students to be successful on a test, I must take a more active role in helping them develop good study techniques. To that end, I plan a test-review time prior to any test date. During this test-review period, I will state the objectives or skills to be covered by the test or quiz, and students must write them down. I insist that students write the following phrase before beginning their list:

For Friday's test, I must be able to . . .

The list, then, might include such items as these:

find the lowest common multiple of a set of numbers.

solve a problem using a graph and an algebraic approach, relating to distance, rate, and time.

After we have the whole list, I introduce practice experiences relating to each of these objectives. I can make the review fun by staging a test-review contest or a team experience. One such approach I call the Test Practice Bingo Contest.

To begin, I have students draw a 4-by-4 grid on their paper. They must then write the numbers 1 through 16 in the grid, in any arrangement they choose. For example, Jamie might place her sixteen numbers as shown in figure 4.

**Figure 4**

| 1 | 13 | 16 | 2 |
|---|----|----|----|
| 9 | 8 | 6 | 10 |
| 11 | 5 | 7 | 12 |
| 3 | 15 | 14 | 4 |

In advance, I have prepared 16 sample test questions on 16 numbered cards (see figure 5). I place the 16 cards into a hat or small box and draw a card from the hat. I read the question; all students work toward the solution. I then read the answer, and have selected students discuss the method of solution. At this point, I read the number written in the corner of the card. Any student who has the correct result may cross out the corresponding number on the grid.

**Figure 5**

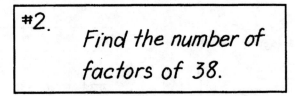

#2.

*Find the number of factors of 38.*

The process is repeated until one or more students have a row, column, or diagonal completely crossed out. Those students are the winners of the contest. To shorten the contest review, you can have fewer cards and give out certain "free numbers" for students to cross out after drawing their grids and before starting the actual review.

The great bonus in this type of contest is that the top students do not always win, because of the "luck factor" in how numbers are placed in the grids. Prizes can be awarded; I use peanuts, NCTM stickers, and the like. (Yes, my students do work for peanuts!)

In addition to in-class test review, I always give homework the night before the test. The assignment is to practice at least one problem or exercise related to each of the objectives listed during our in-class test review. Students must turn in this assignment before I distribute the test on test day. The merit of this homework assignment is that it demands that students do further review for the test on their own.

As you have noted from all of the foregoing, my test content is very public. No surprises, no tricks. My message to the students is that the test is an opportunity for them to show me what they have learned about the important concepts we have covered in the past days.

## *Formatting tests*

The format of the written test sends a strong message to students. Consider a small section of a test I gave some years ago, as shown in figure 6.

Name _____

1. $4bh + 3bl - 2bh - 3bl$     1. _____

2. $-4(5 + s)$     2. _____

3. $3\left(\dfrac{7 + 7r}{7}\right)$     3. _____

4. $6.6d - 3.3D = 3.3$     4. _____

5. Find the value of the expression $C\left(1.000 - \dfrac{0.10}{C}\right)$, when $C = 2$.     5. _____

6. Find the value of $D$ in the equation $D = \dfrac{N}{P} + \dfrac{2000}{P}$ when $N = 64$ and $P = 32$, accurate to four decimal places.     6. _____

**Figure 6.  A test format to avoid.**

What is the message this answer-blank format sends to my students? "I don't have to show my work. I don't have to be organized. All Mr. Johnson wants is the answer. I can work quickly."

Test format is critical! To convey the importance of showing steps and the process for arriving at a solution, it is imperative that my tests provide space for such work, and NOT answer blanks.

Another weakness of this sample test is that it makes no effort to check algebraic skills in a situational and problem-solving mode. Providing a context nearly always makes a problem more interesting to solve—and better prepares students for real life, where problems are rarely encountered as tidy algebraic expressions. Thus, instead of asking my students to simplify $5(3x - 6) - 5(x + 17)$, I should ask:

(a)  If Elena reads $(x + 17)$ books per year and Franklin reads $(3x - 6)$ books per year, and Franklin reads more books per year than Elena, how many more books did Franklin read than Elena in 5 years?

(b)  In order for this expression to make sense, what must the value of $x$ be?

(c)  What values for $x$ don't make sense?

## How a test tests me

I always correct my students' tests. I never have other teachers, aides, or students correct them; test correction is a good time for me to evaluate my instruction. Because I demand that students show the mathematical steps, the process for completing an exercise or solving a problem, I am able to analyze and compile student errors while I'm correcting their papers. This is a great benefit to me. I obtain information to answer the following questions during and after my correction of each set of tests:

- What techniques or skills do my students understand satisfactorily?

- With what techniques or skills do they have the most difficulty?

- What concepts do I need to reteach, or give greater emphasis to, in future class lessons?

- How can I enhance my teaching to achieve greater student success on these most-missed techniques?

- What notes shall I make and file in order to obtain greater success the next time I teach the concepts tested?

- Are there any critical attributes that I underemphasized?


Making sure that homework and testing are positive elements of my math class is an important task for me if I expect to improve student achievement. Assignments and tests should not be anxiety-producing for students, but neither should they be taken lightly. The ideas in this chapter are a step in the right direction; they have helped my students develop a practical attitude and a seriousness of purpose toward both their daily homework and my regular testing routine.

*Chapter Four*

# Motivating by helping students understand the abstract

Anticipating the rough spots

Making variables meaningful

Using counterexamples

**Some things confuse students year after year.**

From our past teaching experiences, you and I have discovered which areas of the concepts we teach are difficult or tricky. That is, we have learned from past classes exactly where students have trouble. If we are truly interested in raising students' achievement, we need to place special emphasis on these areas during the class period. Educator Madaline Hunter would call this "teaching the critical attributes of the content."

## *Anticipating the rough spots*

Here's an example of a rough spot that invariably needs special attention. Students always have difficulty interpreting expressions like these:

$$-x^2 \quad -(x-3)^2 \quad -7^2 \quad -(-3)^2 \quad -(-4^2) \quad -(3^2)$$

Why do these expressions give so many students unnecessary trouble? The form is not emphasized enough in pre-algebra class, nor reemphasized in algebra courses. Too little attention is paid to this *very common form* that appears in many equalities and expressions. I consider this form to be a "critical attribute" of simplification of expressions.

Suppose, for example, I present the following:

Simplify: $-5^2$

Frequently, the immediate answer given is 25. That student believes $-5^2$ means $(-5)^2$. It does not. Yet, do I spend adequate time giving students guided practice in understanding and simplifying expressions of this type? Pointing out such hurdles and providing enough instruction to help students clear these hurdles is a task I must not overlook in my day-to-day teaching. To prevent future errors and misunderstandings in my math class, I must take extra time to practice expressions relating to $-5^2$.

$-5^2$ means $-(5 \cdot 5)$, and should be read "the opposite of the quantity 5 times 5."

$(-5)^2$ means $(-5)(-5)$, and should be read "the opposite of 5, that quantity squared."

I need to point out the order of operations, and state the agreement that the exponent always applies to the smallest meaningful expression to its immediate lower left. However, these agreements are not easily understood, nor remembered, by the typical pre-algebra and algebra student. Stressing the *form* of the expression has proved to be much more successful.

It usually helps to explore the following similar and easily confused forms:

$-5^2 = -(5 \cdot 5)$

$-(5^2) = -(5 \cdot 5)$

$-(5)^2 = -(5 \cdot 5)$

$(-5)^2 = (-5)(-5)$

I emphasize to students that the only form in which $(-5)$ is used as a factor twice is the last case above.

Extra attention to this concept must include giving students practice expressions containing these forms. I ask students to show the definition of subtraction and the definition of exponents, to demonstrate their understanding of these various forms. Examples:

$-3^2 + (-3)^2$

$-(3 \cdot 3) + (-3)(-3)$

$-9 + 9$

$0$

$(-3)^2 - 2^4 - 3$

$(-3)^2 + -(2^4) + -3$

$(-3)(-3) + -(2 \cdot 2 \cdot 2 \cdot 2) + -3$

$9 + -16 + -3$

$-10$

Similar forms occur with variables.

$-x^2$ means $-(x \cdot x)$

$(-x)^2$ means $(-x)(-x)$

Students' understanding of this will bring faster success in solving equations of the form

$-(x - 3)^2 = -16$

$(x - 3) - 3(x - 2)^2 = 12$

or evaluating expressions such as

$-x^2 + 6x + 9$

which leads to graphing parabolas of the form

$$y = -x^2 - 7x + 3$$

In order for students to be successful in dealing with the expression $-5^2$ and other related forms, I must (a) teach the *form* carefully and extensively at the outset, (b) give adequate practice, and (c) provide periodic practice throughout the course. The same is true for other "critical attributes."

## *Making variables meaningful*

Teaching students to use algebraic expressions meaningfully is a goal of all pre-algebra and algebra teachers. However, it is so easy to have the *manipulation* of these expressions become the focus. It certainly happened in my class: I watched as meaningless expressions were added, subtracted, multiplied, divided, and, in general, simplified without any purpose or reason. My students at times didn't even realize they were dealing with numbers. Having students manipulate variables before they understood their use and power led to meaningless drill and practice. It was here that I lost many students.

> *Students are motivated to learn*
> *when they believe they understand*
> *the concept being taught.*
> *When students don't understand,*
> *many of them "turn off"*
> *to the concept being studied.*

I've discovered that I need to present a much more elaborate introduction to the *use* of variables, before I have students start manipulating expressions with variables. The following activities, which I call "pre-simplification exercises," help give these mysterious abstract variables and expressions concrete meaning for students. For some additional ideas and activities, see Appendix B where my article "Making –*x* Meaningful" is reprinted from the NCTM journal *Mathematics Teacher*.

**Pre-simplification exercise 1.**  In this first exercise, I start by placing a number line on the board, asking students to draw a similar line in their notebooks. I then place (–*f*) on the number line as shown below:

Students are then paired up and asked to write down two things they know about the (–*f*) just by looking at the number line. I follow that by asking them to write two things they know about (*f*). With that taken care of, I ask them to write down two things they *don't know* about (*f*) and (–*f*). I then call on two student pairs to discuss their responses to these questions.

   There are many other ways to involve the entire class in this exercise; the important thing is *not* to present it as a worksheet. I want to monitor student responses after each item as I ask them to place the following real numbers on the same real number line:

**1.** 2*f*          **3.** –*f* + 2          **5.** –3*f*

**2.** – ½*f*        **4.** –*f* – 2          **6.** –*g* if *f* < *g* < 0

As a follow-up, we discuss this question:

   Which of these six numbers can be located *exactly* by using simple geometric constructions?

**Pre-simplification exercise 2.**  This exercise works on simple evaluation skills:

   Determine which of the two expressions is larger for any value of *x*:   (*x* + 2) or (*x* – 7).

I encourage my students to approach this by testing some values of *x*, trying at least five replacements for the variable before they form a conjecture. I emphasize the importance of trying positive, negative, and zero values for *x*. Once they have decided that (*x* + 2) is always larger, they use their algebraic skills to check out (*x* + 2) – (*x* – 7): If this is a positive number, then their conjecture is right. A good follow-up question is this:

> By examining the expression $(x + 2) - (x - 7)$, can you justify why $(x + 2)$ will always be larger than $(x - 7)$?

This is an opportunity to use just good old common sense.

**Pre-simplification exercise 3.** This exercise provides additional practice in evaluation skills.

> In the following pairs of expressions, determine which is *always* larger, no matter what the value of the variable(s). Is this always possible to determine? Try at least five replacements for each variable before you make your decision.

| Expressions | | | Larger expression, if possible to determine |
|---|---|---|---|
| $-18$ | or | $-k-4$ | _____ |
| $-7k$ | or | $5k$ | _____ |
| $-k-10$ | or | $-k-1$ | _____ |
| $-3f+1$ | or | $-3f-2$ | _____ |
| $f^3$ | or | $3f^3$ | _____ |
| $3d+1$ | or | $5d+1$ | _____ |

For which of the above expressions are you NOT able to determine which is larger? Why?

**Pre-simplification exercise 4.** Having students explain things in their own words—saying it "in English" instead of "in math"—is a great way of being sure they know what a variable means. In exercises of this type, my students are asked to translate the algebraic expression in the left column into an English phrase, using the information given in the original statement. This ensures that students are putting meaning to expressions before they are asked to simplify them. I insist that they include the units in which the expression is written (feet, miles, hours, etc.).

This type of assignment impresses upon my students that the expressions *do* make sense. The great part is that it is easy to create similar exercises on any topic that will interest and even entertain your students. The following can be put on transparencies or reproducible handouts. I've included the first few answers to "Donuts by the Pound" to show you what I expect.

## Donuts by the Pound

If you buy a pound of these donuts, you get "$y$" of them. Plato purchases "$x$" each day.

Express in your own words the meanings of the following expressions, which contain the variables and constants defined here. Relate each expression to donuts.

Aristotle's
Donut Shop
35¢ each
1000 made daily!

| Expression | Unit(s) of expression | English description of expression as it relates to the story |
|---|---|---|
| 1. $35x$ | ¢ (cents) | Cost in cents of Plato's daily purchase of donuts. |
| 2. $0.35x$ | $ (dollars) | Cost in dollars of Plato's daily purchase of donuts. |
| 3. $\dfrac{x}{y}$ | pounds | # of pounds of donuts Plato purchases per day. |
| 4. $0.35(1000)$ | _____ | _____ |
| 5. $\dfrac{1000}{y}$ | _____ | _____ |
| 6. $7x$ | _____ | _____ |
| 7. $(12)(35)$ | _____ | _____ |

## It's Not Fair!

Seniors at Nicolet High School work twice as many hours on homework per day as freshmen do.

If $y = 2x$ is a true statement for the above situation, what do the following expressions represent?

| Expression | English description |
|---|---|
| **1.** $y$ | _____ |
| **2.** $2x$ | _____ |
| **3.** $7(2x)$ | _____ |
| **4.** $x$ | _____ |
| **5.** $\dfrac{y}{2}$ | _____ |

## How Big is it?

Mr. Johnson's rectangular classroom length is 6 feet more than twice the width.

If $y = 2x + 6$ is a true statement for the above situation, what do the following expressions represent?

| Expression | English description |
|---|---|
| **1.** $x$ | _____ |
| **2.** $y$ | _____ |
| **3.** $2x + 6$ | _____ |
| **4.** $2x$ | _____ |
| **5.** $(x) + (x) + (2x + 6) + (2x + 6)$ | _____ |
| **6.** $2x + 2y$ | _____ |

**Explanations "in their own words" may
try your patience, but the payoff is worth it.**

**Pre-simplification exercise 5.** This exercise, which is to be done without a calculator, ties together the definition of absolute value, the use of variables, and estimation skills. (Answers are hand lettered at right.)

---

### *Absolute Value and Estimation*

If $a > 0$, $|a| = a$ (leave alone)
If $a = 0$, $|a| = a$
If $a < 0$, $|a| = -a$ (take the opposite)

Find the absolute value of each of the following:

1. $\left|-3\right|$               $-(-3)=3$

2. $\left|\pi\right|$               $\pi$

3. $\left|-3y\right|$ if $y < 0$     $-3y$

4. $\left|7x^3\right|$, if $x < 0$     $-(7x^3)$

5. $\left|\sqrt{2}-\pi\right|$         $-(\sqrt{2}-\pi)$

6. $\left|\sqrt{61}-2\pi\right|$      $(\sqrt{61}-2\pi)$

7. $\left|7-\sqrt{51}\right|$       $-(7-\sqrt{51})$

8. $\left|-14-3x\right|$ if $x < -5$    $-14-3x$

In all their different forms, pre-simplification exercises like the foregoing help students see that expressions containing variables do represent actual numbers. They also find that, despite all the mystery about an *x*, they can—with the appropriate information—determine whether such an expression is greater than, less than, or equal to zero.

## *Using counterexamples*

The use of counterexamples is a powerful technique for clarifying a conjecture, theorem, axiom—any mathematical statement, for that matter. In addition, it provides practice in evaluation of expressions and, in some cases, simplification of expressions. It's easy to use this technique: After stating a theorem, for example, I simply ask students to give one example (if one exists) that makes the statement true, and one counterexample (if one exists).

If a counterexample does not exist, I ask the class to justify why they believe the statement is always true. Good discussion results from this type of exercise. I find that it helps students prepare for effectively using the theorems and axioms that they will encounter in algebra and geometry courses. It gives me the chance to work with the meaning of the quantifiers *all, some,* and *none.* In addition, it lets me stress the truth value assignments for an implication, and the method of proving an implication false.

Sometimes I write a statement on the board, informing the students that what I have just written is false. I have each student find a counterexample, then ask them for values that make the statement true (if any). This opening can be a good lead-in to the new concept for the day.

I also use the counterexample technique to be sure they understand definitions of new terms. After giving a definition, I ask students to supply an example to support the definition and be ready to justify their example. I immediately follow up by asking them for a non-example.

Following are some of my favorite statements for which I ask students to find a counterexample:

- All opposites are negative.
- No opposites are positive.
- All subsets are proper subsets.
- All irrational numbers are non-repeating decimals.
- All rational numbers are infinite decimals.
- All integers are repeating decimals.
- No whole numbers are non-positive.
- Some rational numbers are non-repeating decimals.
- All rectangles with equal areas are congruent.
- All rectangles with equal perimeters have equal areas.
- Rectangular solids with equal volume are congruent.
- Rectangles with equal area have equal perimeters.
- Triangles with equal height have equal area.
- Triangles with equal height have equal perimeter.
- All triangles with equal height and base length have equal area.
- Triangles with equal height and base length have equal area.
- Triangles with equal area are congruent.
- The absolute value of all numbers is greater than zero.
- For every real number $(a)$, $|-a| = a$
- For every real number $(a)$, $|a| > -a$
- For every real number $(a)$, $|-a| > a$
- For all real numbers $(a, b)$, if $|a| > |b|$, then $a > b$
- For all real numbers $(a, b)$, $|a + b| = |a| + |b|$
- For all real numbers $(a, b)$, $\sqrt{a+b} = \sqrt{a} + \sqrt{b}$
- For all real numbers $(a, b)$, $a, b \neq 0$, $\dfrac{1}{a+b} = \dfrac{1}{a} + \dfrac{1}{b}$
- For all real numbers $(a, b)$, if $a^2 = b^2$, then $a = b$.
- For all real numbers $(a, b)$, if $a < b$, then $a^2 < b^2$
- For all real numbers $(a, b)$, $\sqrt{a-b} = \sqrt{a} - \sqrt{b}$
- For all real numbers $(a, b)$, $(a + b)^2 = a^2 + b^2$

- For all real numbers $(a, b)$, $ab^2 = (ab)(ab)$
- For every real number $(a)$, $-a^2 = a^2$
- For all real numbers $(a, b, c)$, $b, c \neq 0$, $\dfrac{a+b}{b+c} = \dfrac{a}{c}$
- For all real numbers $(a, b, c)$, if $ac = bc$, then $a = b$

Using counterexamples and the pre-simplification exercises I included in this chapter are both tried and true ways to give real meaning to the abstractions that so commonly trip up our math students. When what they're doing no longer makes sense to them, all motivation to keep going is lost. My efforts as a teacher to make the abstract meaningful for students will help prevent them from performing senseless manipulations, help keep them grounded, help them *truly* understand what's going on.

# Chapter Five

# Motivating through problem-solving experiences

Using "story" situations

Attacking a word problem

Mathematical magic

**Revise story problems as needed to speak to student experience and interest.**

The value of problem solving as the primary approach to teaching mathematics has been amply demonstrated in recent years. The fact is: TEACHING COMPUTATION IN ISOLATION WON'T GET THE JOB DONE! Consider the following:

$90 \div 14 = 6.\overline{4285714}$ (True!)

However, just being able to do the division algorithm will not guarantee that students can apply the algorithm in problem-solving experiences. For example:

1. How many tickets to the Bluegrass Festival can you purchase for $90, if each costs $14? (Is $6.\overline{4285714}$ the answer to this question?)
2. According to school policy, there must be one chaperone for each group of 14 students. How many chaperones are needed for a class of 90 students? (Is $6.\overline{4285714}$ the answer to this question?)
3. What is the cost of one small pizza if Andre has to pay $90 to get 14 for his party? (Is $6.\overline{4285714}$ the answer to this question?)
4. If I run around the track in 14 minutes, how many laps can I make in 90 minutes? (Is $6.\overline{4285714}$ the answer to this question?)

> *Place computation practice*
> *in a problem-solving mode.*
> *We can teach computational skills*
> *at the same time that we teach*
> *problem-solving skills.*

Problem-solving experiences can be the catalyst and umbrella for the learning of many related skills, including evaluation, rational numbers, sketching or drawing diagrams, construction of graphs, translation from English to algebraic expressions, translation of algebraic expressions to English phrases, communication, and estimation. And when these skills are developed, they, in turn, make problem solving more successful. Problem solving leads to skill development, which leads to improved problem solving—as long as the skill is kept in a problem-solving or situational mode.

> *Rewards must go to*
> *the effective problem solvers*
> *with good skill developement and*
> *not to the skill manipulators*
> *with great memories.*

## Using "story" situations

Teaching how to simplify algebraic expressions, as mentioned in the preceding chapter, is one place in the curriculum where it's easy to fall into the trap of "mathematics-as-the-manipulation-of-abstract-symbols." Therefore, even at the very beginning of the simplification unit, I try to keep expressions meaningful by linking them to some simple story or problem situation. Such a story helps give concrete meaning to the variables being used and decreases the likelihood that students will be simply manipulating meaningless expressions for no apparent reason or result.

Thus, for example, instead of Exercise A below, you would accomplish the same end with Exercise B.

| **EXERCISE A** | **EXERCISE B** |
|---|---|
| **Simplify the following:** | **Write the correct expression, in the simplest possible form:** |
| $10(10d) + 5(3d + 1) + 50(2d - 4)$ | The total number of cents in $(10d)$ dimes, $(3d + 1)$ nickels, and $(2d - 4)$ half dollars. |
| $\dfrac{144x - 72}{3}$ | If a room measures $(144x - 72)$ feet in length, the length of the room in yards. |

| **EXERCISE A** *(cont.)* | **EXERCISE B** *(cont.)* |
|---|---|
| $\dfrac{f(3b+2)}{g}$ | The cost of $f$ Norwegian sweaters if $g$ of them cost $(3b+2)$ dollars. |
| $180-(d-5)$ | The measure of angle A if the measure of angle B is $(d-5)$ degrees, and A and B are supplementary angles. |
| $\dfrac{(10d-18)-2(3d)}{2}$ | The width of a rectangle whose perimeter is $(10d-18)$ feet and length is $3d$. |
| $\dfrac{5f+10}{5}$ | The time it takes in hours to travel $(5f+10)$ miles at the rate of 5 miles/hour. |
| $(n-3)+(n-2)+(n-1)$ | The sum of three consecutive odd integers if the largest is $(n-1)$. |
| $(p+25)-(0.12)(p+25)$ | The sale price of Norwegian skis if the original selling price was $(p+25)$ dollars and discount rate being offered is 12%. |

## *Attacking a word problem*

As we all know, word problems are not new to math class. I still use many of the old traditional story problems, but now I follow a more carefully planned approach. Too frequently in the past I rushed straight to the algebraic representation of the problem, and then went into detail on the solution of the equation. I realize now that I had my teaching priorities out of order: I should be spending more time up front, helping students *understand the problem*. The solving of the equation is really secondary to teaching problem-solving skills. Students will model my problem-solving techniques.

I know, because in the past, they were also modeling me—rushing to write the equality on the first step.

In teaching problem solving, I keep in mind these principles:

- Present problems in the future tense; this makes them feel like more genuine problem situations.

- Provide an introduction to the problem at a concrete level.

- Have students use diagrams and manipulatives whenever possible.

- Have students find arithmetic examples to clarify and illustrate the problem.

- Check students' understanding of the problem situation before starting to write expressions and equations using variables.

- At the conclusion of a problem-solving activity, have students write a complete sentence relating the answer to the original question. This writing activity will force a check on the reasonableness of the answer. If students find they have written a sentence that makes no sense, they are motivated to rework the problem.

I often use the overhead projector for presenting problems in class. For such use, I always have masks handy to cover all but the one problem I'm talking about. Displaying only one exercise or problem at a time makes it easier for all students to focus on the same activity. It permits me to control the pace and to monitor each student's progress on a single activity. It also prevents students from doing several problems wrong before receiving help.

When the content is new or difficult, displaying several exercises or the entire transparency to the class can be devastating. Some students, seeing numerous problems displayed all at once, become discouraged. A few will decide immediately that they aren't going to do them all. Others will rush to see how many they can complete in a very short time. Focusing student attention on one issue or problem at a time will keep from overwhelming them and will help them follow along as you lead them through a carefully thought-out plan of attack.

The two sample presentations that follow demonstrate how I help students learn to attack a word problem, step by step, being sure they understand the problem first. The samples are based on standard Algebra I problems on the subject of rate and work. As I walk you through my approach, please keep in mind and notice the following:

- One problem may well take the entire period. I spend as much time as necessary developing activities that help students understand the problem.

- The questions I ask are all given orally, one at a time.

- Students often work in pairs, and develop a joint written response.

- I take time for discussion after each of the questions.

- I make an effort to approach the problems from many different points of view.

- In problem solving, I try to show the connections between many mathematical skills.

## PROBLEM 1

Two boys on bicycles start from the same place at the same time. One rides at the rate of 8 miles an hour, and the other at 5 miles an hour. They go in the same direction. In how many hours are they 15 miles apart?

First, I reword the problem in future tense, trying to make it even the slightest bit more interesting for my students. For example:

## REVISED PROBLEM

Boris Becker and Michael Jordan [or *any current sports figures that might appeal to your students*] are planning to take a bicycle trip together, starting from exactly the same place at exactly the same time. They will follow the same route. However, they don't realize that Jordan rides at the rate of 8 miles an hour, and Becker rides at the rate of 5 miles an hour. If they give up and end the ride after they are 15 miles apart, how many hours will their trip last?

Students may need to review and develop an intuitive feeling for the uniform motion formula: $D = RT$. To this end, I have students make up a situation that exemplifies the formula. Students share their story with their partners.

Suppose a student gives the example: "I walked 2 miles per hour for 3 hours, therefore I walked 6 miles." I can now ask: "If I walked 10 miles at the same rate, how long did it take?" I expect the students to justify their answers. I ask them for two or three examples of uniform motion from their personal experience; I also have them give examples of motion that is not uniform.

Asking appropriate questions to promote understanding of the problem is essential. For the bicycle problem, I use these:

Which cyclist traveled at a faster rate?

Which cyclist went farther?

How do you know that?

By how much?

Who traveled farther before they stopped? Who traveled for a longer time before they stopped?

Have students draw a diagram of the situation at the time the trip was halted, and label each part of the diagram.

Before the students actually start to solve this problem, I introduce intermediate examples for them to calculate:

How far apart are the cyclists after 30 minutes?

How far apart are the cyclists after $1\frac{1}{2}$ hours?

How far apart are the cyclists after 10 hours?

How far does Boris travel in 2 hours?

How far does Michael travel in 2 hours?

After this practice, I ask students to estimate an answer to the original question.

When students have solved the problem algebraically, I might ask the following questions:

How far did Boris travel before they gave up?

What is one statement that summarizes the results of the problem?

Would the time double if they gave up when the distance apart was 30 miles? Justify your answer. Does your answer make sense?

I think it's appropriate, as well, to ask my students if there are any unrealistic conditions related to the problem. For example, could cyclists maintain their respective rates for that length of time? And if they are 15 miles apart, how does each know the other is stopping?

**Graphing it.** Wanting to demonstrate alternate approaches to solving this problem, I ask students to look at it from a graphing point of view. First, I tell them to write an equality representing Michael Jordan's trip in terms of distance, rate, and time, using graph paper to draw the graph, with the vertical axis representing distance, and the horizontal axis representing time. They repeat this with Boris Becker's trip (see figure 7).

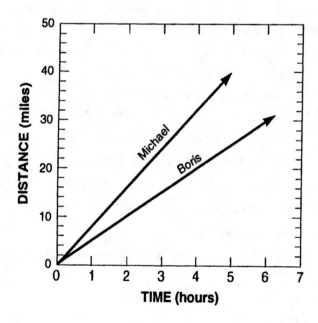

**Figure 7. Graphing the two bicycle trips.**

I then ask the following:

Can you give me three observations regarding the two graphs?

Can you solve the problem by just studying the graphs?

Using the graphs, could you find out how long it would take before Boris and Michael are 50 miles apart? Before they are *n* miles apart?

## PROBLEM 2

If Bob can paint a side of the garage in $4\frac{1}{2}$ hours, and Sally can paint the same side in 6 hours, how long does it take the two of them to paint the same side together?

Again, rewording the problem may add an element of interest.

## REVISED PROBLEM

If Mr. Johnson can wax his car in $4\frac{1}{2}$ hours, and Eric Romanski [*member of my 2nd period class*] can wax the same type car in 6 hours, how long will it take for the two of them, working together, to wax 5 similar cars at next week's Nicolet High School Fund-Raising Car Wash?

Introductory questions like the following can help lead students to an understanding of the situation described in the problem. Remember, I present only one question to students at a time. Students work in pairs to answer them.

Make an estimate of the answer.

Why is $10\frac{1}{2}$ hours not an appropriate estimate?

Why is $5\frac{1}{4}$ hours not an appropriate estimate?

How much of one car is waxed by Mr. Johnson working alone for only 2 hours? Justify your answer.

How much of one car is completed if both Mr. Johnson and Eric work on the same car for 3 hours? 4 hours?

Now, from the results above, make a refined estimate of the answer.

At this point, I guide the entire class through the problem-solving process using charts and diagrams. Then I ask some follow-up questions:

What fractional part of one car will Eric and Mr. Johnson, working together, wax per hour?

Draw the following three graphs on the same plane, expressed in terms of fractional part of a car waxed and time worked:
- one graph of Mr. Johnson working alone
- one graph of Eric working alone
- one graph of Mr. Johnson and Eric working together

From the third graph, can you find how long it will take Mr. Johnson and Eric to wax 5 cars? 6 cars?

How long, working together, will it take them to wax *n* cars?

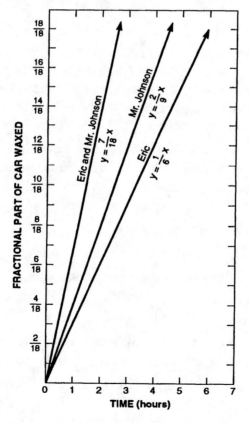

**Figure 8. Graphing the car wash problem.**

These sample presentations (of the bicycle problem and the car waxing problem) show how I promote a thorough understanding of the situation before having students attempt to write an equation. They also show that there is more than one good way to find a solution—graphing, for example, is a good visual alternative to the standard algebraic method.

## *Mathematical magic*

I'm a great believer in the element of surprise as a motivator during math class. For that reason, I've always included "magic tricks" in my problem-solving repertoire.

Making a magical prediction—or doing "mind reading"—can be easily intertwined with practice in simplification of algebraic expressions. I present the mind-reading "tricks," and the students write their own algebraic expressions to help explain them. Here are four of my favorites:

1. Take your favorite number. Subtract 2 from it. Now multiply the number by 3. Now add 6 to it. Now divide the number you have by your favorite number. Your result should be 3. Is it? Why?

2. Take another very fine number. Add 2. Then multiply this number by your original number. Now subtract your original number from this number. Do it again. Your final number should be the square of the original number. Is it? Why?

3. Take your favorite number. Triple it. Subtract 6 from this product. Now divide the number by 3. Now add your original number to this quotient. Now divide by 2. Now subtract your original number from this number. Your final number should be −1. Is it? Why?

4. Select a non-zero integer. Triple it. Subtract 6 from this result. Divide this result by 3. Subtract your original number from this quotient. Add 2 to this result. Your result should be 0. Is it? Explain.

After students try each "trick," ask them to write an algebraic expression that represents the trick. Here is where students get practice simplifying expressions—expressions that they themselves wrote.

**Card tricks.** Mathematical card tricks also provide great hands-on problem-solving situations for my Algebra I class. I've always been interested in magic, but until recently I didn't realize that mathematical card tricks contained very appropriate algebra for the beginning student. Let me illustrate.

### TRICK 1

Given a deck of 52 cards, I will, as the magician, predict the bottom card of a pile of cards that you select. You must follow my directions precisely:

- Shuffle the cards.

- Look at the top card. If it is *10 or higher*, place the card back in the deck. If it is *less than 10*, place it face down and deal off cards on top of this card, counting up until the number 10 is reached. That is, if the top card is a 3, count out 7 more cards to reach the number 10.

- Continue the above process until you can't make any more complete piles. Any remaining cards go to the discard pile, *D*.

- Select any three piles. Place all remaining card piles on the discard pile.

- Turn over two of the three selected piles. At this point, I will magically tell you the card at the bottom of the remaining facedown pile.

**Card tricks—a treasure trove of mathematical problem solving.**

**Solution to the mystery.** The entire magical effect in this card trick is represented by the following simple equation:

$$(11 - B_1) + (11 - B_2) + (11 - B_3) + D = 52$$

where

$B_1$ is the value of the card at the bottom of the first pile,
$B_2$ is the value of the card at the bottom of the second pile,
$B_3$ is the value of the card at the bottom of the third pile,
and $D$ represents the number of cards in the discard pile.

This equation simply states that the sum of the cards in the three piles, plus the number of cards in the discard pile, add up to 52. Solving this equation for $B_3$, we find that:

$$B_3 = D - 19 - B_1 - B_2$$

This equation now tells the magician how to find the value of the bottom card of the third pile. The magician removes from the discard pile 19 cards, plus the sum of the bottom card on the first pile and the bottom card on the second pile. The number of cards remaining will be the value of the bottom card of the third pile.

This type of problem permits students to perform the card trick before writing the model equation that represents the trick itself. Students can discover many other card tricks using this same idea, and can immediately turn to their algebra to discover how the trick is performed.

**The basic principles behind card tricks.** A handy publication from COMAP Publishers, called *Some Card Tricks: Algebra in Disguise,* gives some effective ideas for designing a lesson to introduce card tricks like the one just presented. This booklet points out two basic principles that must be taught before asking students to write the equalities that represent the card mystery.\*

---

\* Thanks to COMAP, Inc. Publisher for their permission to adapt material from *Some Card Tricks: Algebra in Disguise,* by Peter A. Lindstrom, UMAP Unit #560, Modules and Monographs in Undergraduate Mathematics and Its Applications.

PRINCIPLE A: The sum of the numbers of cards in different piles equals the total number of cards in the deck.

To illustrate this principle, suppose that we have a deck of 15 cards and we form two piles, $P_1$ and $P_2$, counting up from the value of the bottom card (as in the card trick), but this time counting until we reach the number 12. Also, instead of burying face cards, we'll give jacks, queens, and kings a value of 10. Assuming that the bottom card of $P_1$ is an 8 and the bottom card of $P_2$ is a king, then there are 5 cards in $P_1$ and 3 cards in $P_2$, as shown in the diagram in figure 9.

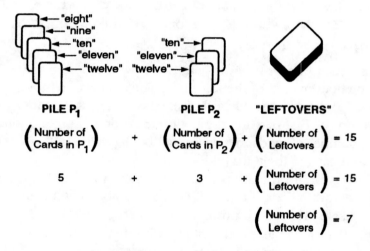

**Figure 9.  Counting up to make the card piles.**

The same diagram can be used to illustrate Principle B, which relates the number of cards in a pile to the values of its top and bottom cards. The following exercises introduce this principle.

**EXERCISE 1.** Of the 5 cards of $P_1$ in the diagram, the bottom card has a value of 8 and the top card as been assigned a value of 12.

(a)  Explain why $12 - 8$ does not give the number of cards in $P_1$.

(b)  Explain why $12 - 10 \neq$ the number of cards in $P_2$.

Before going on to Exercise 2, be sure that you understand Exercise 1.

**EXERCISE 2.** Suppose that in forming a pile of cards, counting values as before, the bottom card has a value of $B$ and the top card has been assigned a value of $T$. Develop a formula for the number of cards in the pile in terms of $B$ and $T$.

The result of Exercise 2 is the second basic principle to be learned.

> PRINCIPLE B: In forming a pile of cards whose bottom card has a value of $B$ and whose top card is assigned the value of $T$, the number of cards in the pile is $(T + 1) - B$.

The following exercise uses both Principle A and Principle B for its solution.

**EXERCISE 3.** Suppose that we have a deck of 36 cards. We form two piles $P_1$ and $P_2$, where a 5 is the bottom card of $P_1$, and a jack is the bottom card of $P_2$. In forming these piles, suppose that we stop counting with 10 for $P_1$ and with 14 for $P_2$. Determine the number of cards left over after the two piles are formed.

If every student brings a deck of cards from home, they can be led to discover the two basic principles through experimentation. This is a hands-on activity that always interests and motivates students.

The following three card tricks from the COMAP booklet are based upon the same principles. I have used them successfully both in class and on tests. (Students are permitted to use a deck of cards when taking the tests.) Other tricks similar to these appear in the same booklet.

**CARD TRICK A.** Suppose that you have a deck of at least 36 cards—but you don't know exactly how many. You form three piles of cards as follows (counting up from the value of the bottom card):

> First pile: Count cards until you reach 10.
> Second pile: Count cards until you reach 11.
> Third pile: Count cards until you reach 12.

Develop a formula, and then a rule, that will tell you the number of cards in the deck in terms of the number of cards left over and the numerical values of the bottom cards of the three piles.

**CARD TRICK B.** You have a standard deck of 52 cards and form four piles of cards as follows (counting up from the value of the bottom card):

First pile: Count cards until you reach 10.
Second pile: Count cards until you reach 11.
Third pile: Count cards until you reach 12.
Fourth pile: Count cards until you reach 13.

Develop a formula, and then a rule, that will tell you the number of cards left over (after the four piles have been formed) in terms of the numerical values of the bottom cards of the four piles.

**CARD TRICK C.** You have a standard deck of 52 cards and form four piles of cards as follows (counting up from the value of the bottom card):

First pile: Count cards until you reach 10.
Second pile: Count cards until you reach 10.
Third pile: Count cards until you reach 11.
Fourth pile: Count cards until you reach 11.

Develop a formula, and then a rule, that will tell you the sum of the bottom cards of the first two piles in terms of the number of cards left over and the sum of the bottom cards of the last two piles.

**Problem solving as a motivator.** It may seem that problem solving is inherently more interesting to students than computation—and it certainly can be, but it can also appear more complicated to them, which can be intimidating. That's why I have demonstrated approaches to problem solving that emphasize *understanding the problem*—through asking careful questions, through a visual approach like graphing, and through hands-on materials like playing cards. Writing the equality to be solved is a step that I allow only after I am convinced that the students understand the conditions of the problem. Why? Because only then can they write an algebraic statement that makes sense. And making math make sense is a key motivator for any student.

*Chapter Six*

# Questions and problems that motivate

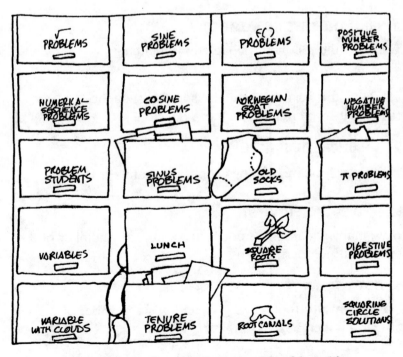

**Every math teacher needs a set of problem files.**

One challenge every math teacher faces is to continually build a large collection of exercises and problems for insertion into class periods when appropriate. An even greater challenge is to *find* these exercises and problems *when you need them.* A file system for each course, updated on a regular basis, aids in this second challenge. When I return from a conference with a new set of problems, or when I locate a great problem in some resource book, I immediately place these problems into existing folders that I have set up for each unit in each class. When I begin my preparation to teach the unit, I go to the appropriate folder, and voilá!—a collection of appropriate problems.

I also file transparencies that I used in previous years, and lists of critical attributes of all the skills to be taught in each unit. My filing system permits me to improve on my teaching of each unit from the previous year; it allows me to begin where I left off, rather than always starting from scratch.

Over the years, I have built up a large collection of exercises and useful problems. This chapter includes 17 of my favorites.

## 1. FIND THE MISSING NUMBER
Consider the following sequence of numbers:

   $0, 3\frac{1}{2}, 8\frac{2}{3}, 15\frac{3}{4}, \ldots$

(a)  Give the next three numbers in this sequence.
(b)  What is the number in the $n$ position?

## 2. A RADICAL QUESTION
Tell me at least three things about this number:   $\sqrt[13]{48}$

## 3. TWO SQUARE ROOTS?
How many square roots does $f$ have, if $f$ is a member of the set of real numbers?

## 4. HOW MANY?
How many $n$th roots does $g$ have if $g$ is a member of the set of real numbers?

## 5. DO I MAKE SENSE?

Is $\sqrt[18]{k}$ a member of the set of real numbers?

## 6. UP, UP AND AWAY

How far can you see from a Pelican Airlines plane in clear weather, if your view in miles equals $1.22 \sqrt{A}$, where $A$ represents your altitude in feet?

(a)  If the Pelican Airlines plane is 35,000 feet above ground, how far can you see?

(b)  If you are a pirate at the top of a 72-foot mast, how far can you see?

(c)  Can you develop the formula $v = 1.22 \sqrt{A}$ using the diagram?

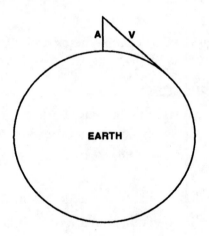

## 7. SCHOOL'S OUT

Joe No-Math states, "There's no time for school!"

| | |
|---|---:|
| Sleep (8 hours a day, total per year) | 122 days |
| Saturdays and Sundays | 104 days |
| Summer vacation | 60 days |
| Meals (3 hours per day) | 45 days |
| Recreation (2 hours a day) | 30 days |
| Total: | 361 days |

Not included are 4 days for illness and 7 school holidays per year. Can you explain what is wrong?

## 8. THE GRAZING BILLY GOAT

Consider the red barn with all doors locked, and the Norwegian goat, shown below.

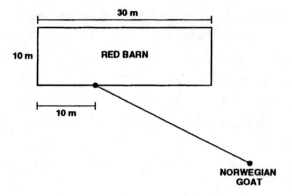

The goat is tied at the end of a 30-meter rope. What is the total grazing area available to the goat (in square meters)?

## 9. THE "HELLO" PROBLEM

Suppose that in my class the first day, I ask that all students walk around and say "hello" to every other student.

- How many "hellos" will I hear if there are 30 students in the class?

- How many "hellos" if there are $n$ students in the class?

This problem can be solved using various techniques, including constructing charts, observing patterns, and sketching. You may recognize its close relationship to the famous Handshake Problem—sometimes it's fun to give the old standbys a new twist.

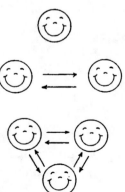

## 10. THE TENNIS BALL PROBLEM

Which is greater, the circumference of a tennis ball, or the height of the standard tennis ball can in which the ball came?

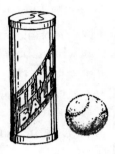

TEACHING NOTE: Have a can and tennis ball on display as you present this problem. The illusion is perfect: The can looks taller than the circumference of the ball. The answer is surprising to most students. Many interesting mathematical explanations can be developed using the tennis balls and their container; the problem can promote discussions of estimation techniques. A similar problem can be designed using three golf balls and their container.

## 11. THE FLOOR TILE PROBLEM

**A.** Consider square floor tiles with blue borders. The Fine Floor Tile Company builds three kinds of tile designs:

- Square tiles with a blue strip on one edge.
- Square tiles with blue strips on adjacent edges.
- Tiles with no strips.

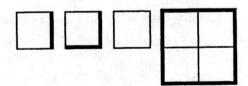

Larger squares of 2 × 2 flooring are built by using four #2 tiles (see diagram).

(a)  Construct and complete a chart showing the number of each type of tile used for squares of flooring 3 × 3, 4 × 4, 5 × 5, and 6 × 6.

(b)  Can you develop a formula for the general case—an $n \times n$ block of flooring, where $n$ is a natural number?

**B.** Suppose that instead of flooring built from squares, we are creating obtuse floors, in which the width of each larger block is $n$ and the length is $(n + 1)$ where $n > 1$.

(a)  Build a chart for the following larger blocks:

    2 × 3        3 × 4        4 × 5        5 × 6

(b)  Can you find formulas for the general case $(n)$ $(n + 1)$ in terms of type of tiles?

**C.** What can you say about the general case for all floors $(n \times m)$ in terms of the number of each kind of tile?

## 12.  IS IT REAL?

Given a real number $a$ as shown on the number line below, find two real numbers between 3 and $a$. Select the smaller, and justify your answer.

## 13. THE FAMILY VACATION PROBLEM

You are on a vacation with your family. Your dad checks into the cost of renting a car for the day. There are only two car rental companies on this island. Here is what he finds out:

| Company | Basic Daily Cost | Additional Charge |
|---|---|---|
| Rent-A-Wreck | $40 | 10¢/mile (100 miles free) |
| Rent-A-Dent | $35 | 15¢/mile (90 miles free) |

Which car should the family rent for the day to minimize costs?

## 14. THE EQUATOR PROBLEM

Put a ring around the equator. Now cut it, enlarge it by 6 feet, and put it back. How far out from the earth will it be? (The earth's radius is 4000 miles.)

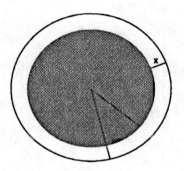

  (a)  A negligible amount.

  (b)  A ladybug might be able to crawl underneath the ring.

  (c)  A chipmunk could run underneath the ring.

  (d)  Your mathematics teacher could crawl underneath the ring.

  (e)  You could drive a riding lawn mower underneath the ring.

## 15. THE TALL WISCONSIN TREE PROBLEM

Paul Bunyan felled two tall trees and left the logs, each 1 mile long, lying end to end. Suppose that his big Blue Ox then moved the logs toward one another, moving each exactly 1 foot. How far above the ground are the logs where they touch?

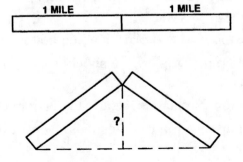

## 16. ASSOCIATED GRAPHS OF SOLUTION SETS

Describe in words the solution set for each of the following. Do not find it. Just tell me about the characteristics, size, etc.

**1.** $5x + 2y = -1$

**2.** $-7x > 2y - 4$

**3.** $4x^2 + 4x + 1 = 0$
(one variable)

**4.** $y = 4|(x + 2)| - 4$

**5.** $3x - 7 = 2(x - 7)$
(one variable)

**6.** $5x^2 + x - 1 = 0$
(one variable)

**7.** $\begin{cases} 3x - 2 + y = 0 \\ 4x + 2y + 1 = 0 \end{cases}$

**8.** $x^2 = 3$
(one variable)

**9.** $y = -7$
(two variables)

**10.** $\begin{cases} 4x - 5 = 2y \\ 4y + 10 = 8x \end{cases}$

**11.** $|x - 2| = 4$
(one variable)

**12.** $(x - 1)^2 + 18 = 0$
(one variable)

## 17. SPECIAL CARD ARRANGEMENTS

Arrange cards numbered 1 through 10 in one pile so that the following "miracle" occurs.

STEP 1.  Take top card and place it at the bottom of the pile.

STEP 2.  Hold up new top card. It should be card number 1. Discard.

STEP 3.  Take top card and place it at the bottom of the pile.

STEP 4.  Hold up new top card. It should be card number 2. Discard.

STEP 5.  Take new top card and place it at the bottom of the pile.

STEP 6.  Hold up new top card. It should be card number 3. Discard.

Keep repeating this process until all cards are used.

(a)  Find an arrangement to achieve the above using 12 cards; using 8 cards; using *n* cards.

(b)  What will always be the top card, no matter how many cards are in the pile?

(c)  What will always be the bottom card?

That's it—17 of my all-time favorites. My suggestion to the reader at this point is to select any or all of the above problems, as suitable for your class, and place them immediately in an appropriate file, ready to use in a forthcoming unit in your math class. Maybe you already have such a file—if not, this is a start. After 33 years, you'll find those files to be a rich resource of motivational problems for your classes, believe me! You should see my files at this point.

# *In conclusion*

In this book, I have shared with you a number of techniques and activities that I believe contribute to raising student motivation, and hence student achievement. Motivated students result not from a single activity or action, but from a blend of many actions by both the teacher and students. Motivated students are the result of a learning atmosphere that is created by:

- Well-planned opening and closing activities.
- Letting students know I want to know if they know.
- Being a TBWA teacher, and monitoring consistently the progress of students during the class period.
- Using a refined art of questioning—one that directs all questions to all students.
- Focusing on student activities rather than teacher activities, and encouraging students to work and communicate together.
- Making the purpose of all activities very clear.
- Making homework an essential part of each lesson.
- Modifying tests, and test procedures.
- Weaving problem solving throughout the curriculum.
- Appealing to students' interests.

May the ideas in this book also aid in motivating your students to achieve!

## *Appendix A*

# Lesson planning guide

The following outline is a useful lesson planning guide as I design each of my class periods. It provides great flexibility, yet protects me from incomplete or insufficient planning. It is a reminder to me to focus on preparing a class that *motivates* students to learn.

Course: _____

Unit:_____

Date/hour of class: _____

1. Student objectives for the class period:

2. Opening activities (first 2 minutes) for students:

3. Order of instructional activities:

4. Evaluation procedures to be used during the class period (checking for understanding):

**5.** Details on how students' understanding of and success on homework will be checked:

**6.** Details on assignment for tomorrow—how it relates to today's objectives:

**7.** Check those content areas from the *NCTM Standards* that will be included in the lesson:

__ Problem Solving     __ Geometry/Synthetic Perspective

__ Communication     __ Geometry/Algebraic Perspective

__ Reasoning     __ Mathematical Structures

__ Connections     __ Statistics

__ Trigonometry     __ Probability

__ Algebra     __ Discrete Mathematics

__ Functions     __ Concepts of Calculus

**8.** Check those techniques that will be incorporated into the class period:

__ Use of manipulatives

__ Use of computer

__ Working in pairs

__ Student presentation

__ Use of calculators

__ Questioning techniques (high level)

__ Cooperative learning activities

**9.** Closing activity (last 2 minutes) after the assignment has been given:

*Appendix B*

# Making –x meaningful

The following is reprinted with permission from the *Mathematics Teacher,* copyright 1986 by the National Council of Teachers of Mathematics.

How do your algebra students read the symbol $-x$? Common responses are "negative $x$," "minus $x$," "the opposite of $x$," or "the additive inverse of $x$." The most common response is "negative $x$." But are all these responses meaningful? Definitely not! In fact, the first two responses are very misleading, if not incorrect. In many classrooms, teachers are quite careful to name a real number less than zero (or to the left of zero on the real-number line) a *negative number.* Students quite easily grasp the meaning of the phrase *negative number.* But suddenly we bring out the expression $-x$ and read it "negative $x$"! Trouble begins. Students immediately assume that this symbol stands for a number less than zero simply because its verbal name contains the word *negative.*

If you don't believe that "negative $x$" is a misleading name, try writing the symbol $-x$ on the board and ask your students. how it relates to zero on the number line. You will probably hear a resounding cry, "To the left of zero!"

Too many students do not understand that if $x$ is a real number, $-x$ could be positive, negative, or zero, and that more information is needed before a decision can be made. Students are so inured to the use of the word *negative* and the definition of a negative number that they do not appreciate the meaning of the expression $-x$. Students do appreciate, however, that additive inverses or opposites do not have to be negative. We would probably be better off if we taught our students to read the expression $-x$ as "the opposite of $x$." In fact, the main point of this article is that discontinuing the use of the term *negative* would be beneficial.

If we do not read $-x$ as "the opposite of $x$," the problem is further complicated when we teach the definition of absolute value. Though the concept of absolute value can be defined in many homespun ways, some are confusing and often incorrect, for example: "The absolute value can be found by dropping off the sign." That idea is deadly. If $b$ is less than zero, then $|b|$, in this instance, equals $-b$. No sign was chopped off. In fact, one was added. When it comes to the definition of such terms as *absolute value,* a mathematically sound definition is necessary. See definition 1.

DEFINITION 1. For all real numbers $a$, (1) if $a = 0$, $|a| = 0$, so $a$ remains unchanged; (2) if $a > 0$, $|a| = a$, so $a$ remains unchanged; (3) if $a < 0$, $|a| = -a$, so the result is the opposite of $a$.

This definition is difficult for students to understand. First, they must know the size of the real number in relation to zero. Secondly, the student must understand that $-x$ is simply a symbol for the "inverse of $x$" and obeys the property of trichotomy. That is, $-x$ could be positive, negative, or zero. If, for example, a student is asked to define the "absolute value of $a$" where $a$ is less than zero, it follows that the $|a|$ equals $-a$. But for students who believe that a negative sign must be dropped to obtain the absolute value of a number, or for those who do not appreciate that in this instance "$-a$" is really a positive number, correctly applying the definition of absolute value to this expression will be difficult.

Students will do well on the examples that follow if they have a good understanding of the definition of absolute value and if they understand that the symbol $-x$ represents the inverse of $x$.

**EXERCISE:** Simplify the following:

1.    $|-b^3|$, if $b < 0$

   (*Answer:* $-b^3$, because $(-b^3) > 0$)

2.    $|-3 -x|$, if $x > 0$

   (*Answer:* $-(-3 -x)$, because $(-3 -x) < 0$)

3.    $|-b| + |-b|$, if $b < 0$

   (*Answer:* $-2b$, because $(-b) > 0$)

4. $|3b|$, if $b < 0$

(*Answer:* $-3b$, because $3b < 0$)

Expressions with variables should be introduced when the concepts of absolute value are taught in first-year algebra. Using only constants in your examples may lead to students' using poor techniques to simplify absolute value expressions. That is, students may be able to get the correct answer but never realize that they do not understand the definition.

Practice in determining the size of the expression prior to teaching an algebraic definition of absolute value will help make the definition more meaningful. See the [following activity] for a series of questions that will help students' understanding of $-x$.

We should read the expression $-x$ as "the opposite of $x$" and insist that students do the same. The correct reading of this expression should begin in the early grades because an incorrect reading of the symbol is not easily changed. A student's use of "negative $x$" complicates and confuses the concepts that an algebra teacher must teach. It's time we tell it like it is!

## ACTIVITY: UNDERSTANDING −X

Consider the following questions:

1. What is the value of the expression $(x - 6)$ if $x < 0$?

   a. Always less than 0
   b. Always greater than 0
   c. Zero
   d. Sometimes less than and sometimes greater than zero

On a number line, place $(x - 6)$ to the left of zero:

That is, if $x < 0$, then $(x - 6) < 0$.

$(x - 6)$ is a negative number for any value of $x$ that is negative.

2. Determine the sizes of the following expressions given the information about the values of the variables. Place a check in the appropriate column.

| Expression | Value of variable | Less than zero | Equal to zero | Greater than zero |
|---|---|---|---|---|
| 1. $x^3$ | $x < 0$ | | | |
| 2. $x^2 + 6$ | $x > 0$ | | | |
| 3. $x^2 + 6$ | $x < 0$ | | | |
| 4. $x^2 + 6$ | $x = 0$ | | | |
| 5. $-3x$ | $x < 0$ | | | |
| 6. $5y$ | $y < 0$ | | | |
| 7. $-5x + y$ | $x < 0, y > 0$ | | | |
| 8. $(x - 14)^2$ | $x < 0$ | | | |
| 9. $(x - 14)^2$ | $x > 0$ | | | |
| 10. $(x - 14)^2$ | $x = 0$ | | | |
| 11. $-f$ | $f < 0$ | | | |
| 12. $-f^2$ | $f > 0$ | | | |
| 13. $-f + (-g)$ | $f < 0, g < 0$ | | | |
| 14. $f^3 + (-2g)$ | $f > 0, g < 0$ | | | |
| 15. $-3x^2$ | $x > 0$ | | | |
| 16. $-2(x - 1)^2$ | $x < 0$ | | | |

3.  Given the following information, place the nonzero real numbers $-f$, $g$, and $h$ on the proper side of zero and in the proper order on a real-number line. Assume the following: $f < 0$, $f < g$, $g < 0$, $-h > -f$, $-h > 0$, and $h < f$.

0

Using this information, decide on which side of zero the following numbers are located:

| Expression | Left | Right |
|---|---|---|
| $f^3$ | | |
| $f - g$ | | |
| $-g^2$ | | |
| $h^2$ | | |
| $h + g$ | | |
| $(-g) + (-f)$ | | |